Procedural Justice and the Fair Trial in Contemporary Chinese Criminal Justice

Governance and Public Policy in China

Volumes published in this Brill Research Perspectives title are listed at *brill.com/rpg*

Procedural Justice and the Fair Trial in Contemporary Chinese Criminal Justice

By

Elisa Nesossi and Susan Trevaskes

BRILL

LEIDEN | BOSTON

Originally published as Volume 2(1–2) 2017, in *Governance and Public Policy in China*, DOI:10.1163/24519227-12340003.

The Library of Congress Cataloging-in-Publication Data is available online at http://catalog.loc.gov
LC record available at http://lccn.loc.gov/2018950593

Typeface for the Latin, Greek, and Cyrillic scripts: "Brill". See and download: brill.com/brill-typeface.

ISBN 978-90-04-38637-2 (paperback)
ISBN 978-90-04-38638-9 (e-book)

This book is printed on acid-free paper and produced in a sustainable manner.

Contents

Author Biographies

Elisa Nesossi
is an Australian Research Council Early Career Research Fellow at the Australian Centre on China in the World (Australian National University). Her research interests include: contemporary Chinese law, Chinese criminal justice, human rights in China, Chinese legal history, comparative human rights law and comparative criminal justice. She is the author of *China Pre-Trial Justice. Criminal Justice, Human Rights and Legal Reforms in Contemporary China* (Wildy, Simmonds & Hill Publishing, 2012). Her co-edited volumes include *The Politics of Law and Stability in China* (Edward Elgar Publishing, 2014), *Legal Reforms and Deprivation of Liberty in Contemporary China* (Routledge, 2016) and *Justice: The China Experience* (Cambridge University Press, 2017).

Susan Trevaskes
is Professor of Chinese Studies in the School of Humanities, Languages and Social Sciences at Griffith University, Australia. Her China-related research interests include criminal courts, policing serious crime, the death penalty, justice and the political nature of criminal justice in China. She has published sole-authored books in the area of Chinese criminal justice studies: *Courts and Criminal Justice in Contemporary China* (Lexington Press, 2007), *Policing Serious Crime in China: from 'strike hard' to 'kill fewer'* (Routledge, 2010) and *The Death Penalty in Contemporary China* (Palgrave Macmillan, 2012). Her co-edited volumes include *The Politics of Law and Stability in China* (Edward Elgar Publishing, 2014), *Legal Reforms and Deprivation of Liberty in Contemporary China* (Routledge, 2016) and *Justice: The China Experience* (Cambridge University Press, 2017).

Procedural Justice and the Fair Trial in Contemporary Chinese Criminal Justice

Elisa Nesossi
Australian National University
elisa.nesossi@anu.edu.au

Susan Trevaskes
Griffith University
s.trevaskes@griffith.edu.au

Abstract

This review examines the literature on procedural justice and the fair trial over the past two decades in the People's Republic of China. Part 1 gives a wide-angle view of the key political events and developments that have shaped the experience of procedural justice and the fair trial in contemporary China. It provides a storyline that explains the political environment in which these concepts have developed over time. Part 2 examines how scholars understand the legal structures of the criminal process in relation to China's political culture. Part 3 presents scholarly views on three enduring problems relating to the fair trial: the presumption of innocence, interrogational torture, and the role of lawyers in the criminal trial process.

Procedural justice is a particularly pertinent issue today in China, because Xi Jinping's *yifa zhiguo* 依法治国 (governing the nation in accordance with the law) governance platform seeks to embed a greater appreciation for procedural justice in criminal justice decision-making, to correct a politicolegal tradition overwhelmingly focused on substantive justice. Overall, the literature reviewed in this article points to the serious limitations in overcoming the politicolegal barriers to justice reforms that remain intact in the system, despite nearly four decades of constant reform.

Keywords

China – fair trial – governance – politicolegal culture – procedural justice

 | DOI:10.1163/9789004386389_002

Introduction

Rule of law, a complex and multifaceted concept, is central to debates about law and governance in both democratic and authoritarian political systems. Authorities in both political contexts cast it as an ideal of irrefutable importance to the stable governance of a country, creating the framework on which both legislative and justice system procedures are conceived, conducted, and reformed. Crucial in many declarations and political discussions about achieving the rule of law is the right to a fair trial, to protect individuals from the unlawful and arbitrary curtailment or deprivation of other basic rights and freedoms. As a fundamental norm of international human rights law, this right is recognized internationally by authorities as one of the key guarantees of criminal, civil, and administrative proceedings.

In common law settings, numerous rights are subsumed under the umbrella of the fair criminal trial, and these apply to pretrial and trial proceedings, appeal, and sentencing. The idea of the fair trial in common law systems was historically associated with the development of constitutional rights. Around 150 years ago, the focus of the fair trial concept shifted from a general commitment to improving the trial process overall to one connected specifically with individual rights (Langford 2009). By contrast, in the People's Republic of China (PRC), because the system draws heavily on a civil law tradition, combined with aspects of socialist law (and is ruled by the Chinese Communist Party [CCP]), the party-state's focus on improving fairness in criminal trials has remained squarely on reforming the trial. The stated motivation is to enhance "judicial justice and efficiency" (*sifa gongzheng yu xiaolü* 司法公正与效率) of the criminal justice system as a whole, rather than to pursue a discrete commitment to protecting individual rights.[1] In China, authorities often refer to the reform goal of improving "judicial justice." According to Chinese scholars, this entails the pursuit of procedural justice as part of the overall aim of facilitating and obtaining a fair substantive outcome. Conceived in this way, judicial justice embodies aspects of both the concepts that Western scholars refer to as procedural justice and substantive justice, with a definitive emphasis on achieving substantive justice outcomes (Li Y 2003).[2]

1 For evidence of the importance of "judicial justice and efficiency as guiding principles of judicial reform," see any of the numerous Supreme People's Court (SPC) Work Reports Reports beginning in the late 1990s. For instance, see the then—SPC President Xiao Yang's work report to the National People's Congress in 2001 at http://www.china.com.cn/chinese/law/117201.htm. On the current use of judicial justice terminology in the Xi Jinping era, see Xinhua 2017a, 2017b. On use of judicial justice terminology in official political statements, see Xi 2015.

2 Western concepts of substantive and procedural justice are discussed in more detail in Part 1 below.

In any modern legal system, crimes are prosecuted on the basis of an understanding that a criminal act is socially harmful. In China, state authorities generally assess the nature and extent of harm that can be attributed to a particular criminal behavior in terms of the degree of "social harm" (*shehui weihai* 社会危害) that the behavior has inflicted—that is, harm not only to the individual victim(s) but also to socialist social relations that may affect Chinese society at large (Lin 1992; Zhao and Chen 2013). In a similar vein, party authorities recognize the political importance of judicial justice because they see that it supports the broad sociopolitical goals of state development and social stability (Wang L 2007). Judicial justice and much of the rhetoric around it concerning due process therefore contribute to achieving the overarching reform goals of modernization and development.

This review article draws together key analyses in the Western and Chinese scholarly literature concerning procedural justice and the fair trial in China. It seeks to identify how this field of scholarship variously interprets changes in procedural justice and in the fair trial and rules and rights associated with it in the criminal process.[3] Our review period is roughly the past two decades, during which the party-state has begun to reposition law systemically in relation to national governance under the banner of *yifa zhiguo*—that is, from when President Jiang Zemin first espoused this in the late 1990s to current reforms in the name of *yifa zhiguo* under President Xi Jinping. Here we observe in the literature that, although norms and practices of procedural justice are drawn into the Chinese justice system, this system is structured for substantive law to enable overarching receptivity to central party-state policies. Because the Chinese regime portrays itself as a dictatorship of the people, the CCP that represents this dictatorship allows the legal system to institutionalize only the extent of limited accountability that the party deems required by procedural justice. In this context, the concept of a fair trial in China may be understood through the question "fair for whom?" Politicolegal party authorities are guided by appraisal of the political, economic, and social imperatives that inform national policy, especially by concern for the country's social stability, which is influenced by all three and is intrinsic to the party's hold on governance. Fairness is thus more a matter for the collective than for an individual.

3 This article reviews only first-instance criminal trials, not appeals or procedural justice in the area of administrative punishment. For analyses of appeals, see Kuang and Liang 2015a, 2015b. For analysis of administrative punishment see Biddulph 2017; Biddulph et al. 2017b. On reforms to the criminal justice system to accommodate minor offences after abolition of the re-education through labor system in 2014, see Biddulph 2016, 2017; Biddulph et al. 2017a.

We begin this review with the sociopolitical context that generates and sustains the concepts of procedural justice. We are guided by legal scholar Perry Keller's insightful observation of Chinese socialist law over two decades ago, which remains germane to all discerning studies on Chinese criminal justice today. He observed that what party authorities for decades have perceived as the building blocks of certainty and predictability in law originate not from narrow and formalist expositions of legal rules but from their understanding of the broader ideological context of socialist development. The dominant idea underpinning the operation of China's criminal law process is "the instrumental use of law and *its essential openness to its context*" (Keller 1994, p. 754; emphasis added). This means context as perceived, understood, and appreciated by central party authorities. Moves to order and legitimize the criminal trial in the PRC have therefore rested on the dominant party-state understanding of the trial's utility to the top-priority national agendas, which are connected to state development and social stability and, ultimately, to the stability of the party itself.

Given the importance of this contextual lens, we find that the most compelling studies of the criminal law process in China situate the development of legal concepts within the sociopolitical context in which they operate. The most insightful studies are those that follow the general spirit of Donald Clarke's work (2003), which critiques the teleological tendency to see law in the PRC as moving toward a certain predictable evolutionary end—a "thin" or socialist rule of law, for instance. Moreover, we argue that studies that critique China's justice system using the yardstick of liberal democratic values are equally unhelpful in understanding the nexus between justice and politics in China today. In contrast, the scholarly works that we include in this review article show that, in post-Mao China, how party leaders create legitimating discourses around what they perceive to be a just and fair criminal trial is highly conditional upon the goals of the party's overall nation-building platforms. This is the case from the Jiang-era *yifa zhiguo* discourse through Hu Jintao's Harmonious Society (*hexie shehui* 和谐社会) and Stability Maintenance (*weihu wending* 维护稳定) and remains so today under Xi's *yifa zhiguo*. We find that the most insightful contributions to knowledge see the nexus between political platforms and the operations of criminal justice as symbiotic. The analyses most useful for understanding Chinese law are those view that national governance and reform platforms with a wide-angle lens, recognizing them as the vital foundation of party authorities' intentions to improve due process and crime control measures. Studies that privilege context tend not to use as their starting point the question of individual rights or the lack thereof to frame their argument for or against rights deprivation, nor do they uncritically treat legal reform as evidence of "progress" toward some form of a socialist or liberal rule of law. Rather, they see analysis of the sociopolitical utility of justice and fairness discourse and how it is used by the party-state for higher political purposes as the most effective way to critically understand and evaluate the significance of procedural justice and the fair trial in China.

Our review of this literature moves from the broad context to the particular, turning first to contemporary history, then to the criminal procedural system and how it accommodates both crime control and due process goals, and finally specific laws, principles, and rights that affect the prospect for a fair criminal trial. Part 1 presents a wide-angle view of the key political events and developments that have shaped the experience of procedural justice and the fair trial in contemporary China, locating these themes within a storyline that explains the political environment in which they have been developed over the past two decades. The context is the dynamic interplay between reform, economic development, and social stability that has driven party authorities to prioritize stability preservation as a key goal underpinning judicial justice and judicial efficiency reforms. In Part 2, we examine how sociolegal scholars understand the legal structures of the criminal process in relation to China's political culture. We consider what some observers have characterized as the "policy-implementing" structure of the criminal process in China, which has set the ground rules for how judicial decision-makers determine culpability. In Part 3, we further narrow the lens to specific debates about and reforms of fair trial provisions in the law, which have remained particularly problematic in the eyes of both Chinese and Western scholars. We consider how the literature has approached three enduring concerns from the late 1990s: the presumption of innocence, interrogational torture and related discussions on evidence, and criminal defense.

1 The Justice Storyline

1.1 *Procedural Justice and Accountability in an Authoritarian Context*

In any legal system, concepts such as procedural justice and due process are developed over time in keeping with governance objectives beneficial to the political structures that define and circumscribe their operation. How and why governing bodies develop rules for procedural justice as a way to produce and maintain social cohesion is the subject of scholarly debate in both authoritarian and democratic contexts. In the Western-liberal fields of law and social science, procedural justice scholars have long argued that a shared commitment to the value of due process promotes harmony and cooperation and is thus a bedrock for sustained social stability. When there is shared acceptance of the principles of a level playing field, due process such as administrative or judicial review, and appeal, members of society are likely to accept as legitimate the decisions of legal or government actors, thus creating a stable social environment. Broad public acceptance of the value of procedural rules governing due process is crucial for shaping the way in which modern societies deal with pluralities and conflicts of interest (MacCoun 2005; Tyler 1990; Tyler and Lind 2001).

In both authoritarian and democratic contexts, procedural justice is commonly defined in contrast to substantive justice. Substantive justice is generally construed as an understanding that a political, administrative, or adjudicatory decision is based on what an appointed decision-maker deems inherently fair, because such a decision-maker has the capacity to deliver what the object of the decision-making deserves (Walker et al. 1979). Scholars such as Tyler (1990) and Walker et al. (1979) recognize procedural justice not as a substitute for substantive justice but as a way of creating a level playing field for decision-making through the guarantee of checks and balances to secure impartiality and, ultimately, a just outcome. Conceived this way, procedural justice entails limiting the capacity of decision-makers to rely solely or predominantly on their own understanding of what is fair. Broad societal acceptance that procedural justice is needed in all areas of governance enables and requires authorities to codify in law structures for enforcing due process provisions to control arbitrary decision-making and abuse of power at each step of decision-making, leading up to a final legal, administrative, or governmental outcome. Through shared commitment to due process principles, democratic societies comprising citizens with diverse social values and political and economic interests—that is, pluralistic societies—can cohere and remain socially stable despite those competing values and interests. As Joshua Rosenzweig suggests, over time, along with social change comes a change in thinking about justice, one that highlights the importance of adhering to adjudicatory or governance processes with meaningful checks and balances on power. He explains:

> As societies evolve and become more diverse and pluralistic, consequentialist versions of justice—such as utilitarianism's promotion of the greatest good for the greatest number—begin to break down in the absence of clear consensus about common values and goals. Part of what allows pluralist societies to continue to cohere despite their diversity is a shift toward thinking about justice in procedural terms that enable the conflicts that inevitably arise in such societies to be resolved through

> political and adjudicatory processes based on clear norms reflecting agreed-upon principles that emphasise fairness, equality and respect for individual dignity.
>
> ROZENZWEIG 2017, p. 29

A society with a political system that is open to resolving conflict and mediating divergent values and interests through a shared acceptance of political, administrative, and adjudicatory rules of a decision-making process can avoid both legitimacy crises in the political systems and constant threats to social and political instability. When power holders in the types of societies identified by Rosenzweig are subject to the scrutiny of robust and independent procedural oversight, the institutions under their control have a benchmark for fair decision-making that is recognized and generally agreed upon by both those who govern and those who are governed. In short, it creates trust in the law and the legal institutions that implement law. But, as Rosenzweig points out, if a society (through those who control a political system) rejects the importance of accommodating diverse values and ideas about fairness and justice, individuals whose vision of justice conflicts with authorities who control the political system will eventually seek expression of their contrasting views through alternative means, such as protest and dissent. These alternative means of attaining justice "have the potential to become the source of political crisis" (2017, p. 29).

The importance of procedural accountability—limiting the capacity of decision-makers to rely solely on their understanding of, and power to decide, what is and is not fair—is accepted as an essential element of governance not only in democratic societies but also in most authoritarian regimes. However, these two system types differ crucially in how public accountability should operate to limit the exercise of power. In China, the very nature of the regime as a so-called dictatorship of the people has meant that the CCP that represents this dictatorship can and does allow only the limited and self-serving development of accountability rules. Party authorities commonly rationalize constraints on both public debate and contestation over what forms and structures accountability should take with the claim that the party and the broad masses of the people it represents already share a vision of fairness and that, consequently, the interests of the party and of the people are as one (Ding 2017). This rationale serves to subvert issues about accountability that could be recognized as "injustice" in society, thus closing down debate and decision-making processes to alternative visions of justice that could compete with the interests of the party. In this political context, accountability mechanisms are developed to protect against abuse of power only insofar as they do not interfere with or challenge the legitimacy of the governing party or its representatives in government and legal institutions.

In China's politicolegal (*zhengfa* 政法) sphere, this limited accountability is supplemented by a high degree of party-state coercion. Because party-state authorities limit the development of procedural guarantees, preserving social stability inevitably relies ever more on state coercion to silence public debate about justice and to deal with dissent from the uneven contest between parties in a dispute, from uneven access to justice or from abuse of power. This scenario is not unique to China. Comparative law scholars who work on rule-of-law issues in authoritarian regimes focus their analysis on the connection between low levels of government accountability and high levels of government coercion (Karstedt 2013; Krygier 2011).[4] Susanne Karstedt notes that this low-accountability high-coercion characteristic circumscribes

> a range of institutional settings through which non-democratic regimes seek to consolidate, claim legitimacy, exert control, and solicit compliance. This institutional space in non-democratic regimes is defined by different levels of accountability and coercion, and by specific mechanisms and institutional designs that allow for making officials accountable or target coercion against specific groups.
>
> 2013, p. 131

Indeed, the central issue that dominates our particular field of criminal justice studies—the Chinese system—is the question of how to best articulate this accountability—coercion dynamic and the changes in it over time. Because we claim that concepts such as procedural justice are developed within the political structures that define and circumscribe their operation, we recognize the most compelling exegeses in our field to be those that locate the accountability—coercion dynamic of this criminal justice system within the overall political storyline of the party's top priority quests—for national modernization and rejuvenation and securing its own position of governance.

Here in Part 1, we set the scene before taking a more detailed look at the scholarly literature on the criminal process and fair trial by presenting the general threads of this storyline, which many scholarly accounts of the criminal process in contemporary China generally acknowledge. We discuss how, over the past few decades, politicolegal authorities have articulated and responded

4 For an examination of accountability and legitimacy in democratic criminal justice settings, see Bottoms and Tankebe 2012.

to changes in a society increasingly fraught with crime and dissent at every major turn of accelerated economic growth. Both the criminal process and the administrative punishment regime deal directly with the social fallout of rapid economic development through their role in containing crime and dissent (Biddulph 2007, 2015). In turn, China's economic modernization drive has profoundly shaped the development of criminal procedure reform. We articulate this symbiotic relationship through examining interplay among the three moving parts that as top national goals have been instrumental in this two-decade period of breakneck modernization: institutional reform, economic development, and social stability. We base this storyline on themes in the literature that we find particularly helpful for understanding the three moving parts of China's modernization drive: the political imperative to prosecute and punish malefactors to protect social stability; the party's understanding of the connection between reform, development, and stability; and efforts to reassert centralized party control to prevent abuse of power, corruption, and miscarriages of justice.

1.2 *Asserting the Political Imperative to Prosecute and Punish*

In any modern state, criminal procedure law is directly related to the perceived need for the state to exercise punitive power on behalf of its citizens. The imperative to prosecute and punish illdoers is always linked to state power because it relies on the concept of a state's legitimate right to exercise power over defendants to benefit or protect its citizens. Even early scholarship on post-Mao justice noted that this political obligation extends well beyond benefiting or protecting citizens, as the PRC's first Criminal Procedure Law (CPL), in 1979, explicitly connected that law's function to sustaining the people's democratic dictatorship for advancing socialist development (Baum 1986; Leng and Chiu 1985).[5] The amended CPL in 2012 continues to uphold this vision, with Article 1 stating that the criminal process operates "to ensure correct enforcement of the Criminal Law, punish crimes, protect the people, protect national security and public security, and maintain the order of socialist society."[6]

5 The People's Republic had no formal criminal law or criminal procedural law before 1979. For a comprehensive outline of the Mao-era system, see Cohen 1968.

6 The CPL enforces the main provisions of the Criminal Law (CL), which, according to Article 2 of CL (1997), are to: use criminal punishments to fight against all criminal acts to defend the security of the state, defend the political power of the people's dictatorship and socialist system, protect property owned by the state and property owned collectively by the working people, protect the citizens' privately owned property, protect the citizens' rights of the person and their democratic and other rights, maintain public order and economic order, and safeguard the smooth progress of the socialist revolution and socialist construction.

These tasks have been the bedrock of criminal justice for nearly 40 years since the reform and opening-up era began in 1979.[7] This is not simply because the law requires it but also because in the party's interpretation of how to manage breakneck economic growth and social change through the marketization process, criminal justice policies must address short-term concerns about maintaining social stability, as they affect the prospects for long-term and sustained institutional reform. The open door reforms signaled by the third plenum of the eleventh party congress in late 1978 were intended to engineer a significant shift in the justice system's approach to justice administration in the wake of the far-reaching political, economic, and social transformation announced by the then-supreme leader Deng Xiaoping (Baum 1986; Leng and Chiu 1985). Changes in the organization of the criminal law process, including the criminal trial, were the result of a compromise among different institutional actors and were intended to be multidimensional. In 1979, the focus shifted from closed criminal trials to public trials, new criminal and civil divisions were set up in courts to deal specifically with appellate cases, and courts throughout the country initiated discussions on trial procedure (Baum 1986; Leng and Chiu 1985). In the early months after the promulgation of the PRC's first CPL in 1979, legal training was mounted across the country for those working in courts and prosecution, and, as a symbol of a new post-Mao commitment to accountability building, courts began to redress cases from the Cultural Revolution (Baum 1986; Leng and Chiu 1985). But these positive accountability developments occurred precisely when courts began to launch coercive anti-crime campaigns, including conducting mass sentencing rallies to frighten criminals and educate the masses, under the party-state's "Strike Hard" (*Yanda* 严打) anti-crime policy (Bakken 2000; Tanner M 1999; Tanner H 2000; Trevaskes 2007). This began a nearly four-decade-long pattern in which the party has progressively developed accountability measures within the criminal law system, while maintaining a coercive crime control politicolegal culture.

This nexus between accountability and coercion is understood in various ways in scholarship on China's CPL. Guo Zhiyuan notes that Chinese scholarly accounts of CPL reform have commonly articulated this as a nexus between crime control and human rights. Here the term "human rights" has often served as a surrogate for what Western criminal justice scholars would describe as due process provisions. As Guo observes:

7 Indeed, they were a hallmark of the system in the 1950s. For a detailed account of criminal justice in this era, see Cohen 1968. For a history of the political nature of policing in this period, see Dutton 2005.

> CPL reform is closely entwined with maintaining social stability in any jurisdiction; by its nature a criminal justice system is to deal justly with crimes and extreme anti-social behaviors that threaten social stability to maintain social order. In the history of modern criminal procedure we can perceive a gradual, sometimes interrupted, but obvious shift in understandings of criminal justice away from overwhelming emphasis on punishment toward emphasis on rights protection. All along, criminal procedure has continued to pursue the political goal of social stability through just punishment of criminals to prevent socially disruptive crime. There is a consensus among Chinese academics that the CPL has dual goals: crime control and due process (or human rights protection as Chinese scholars prefer to call it). The former requires the CPL to be effective in punishing actual offenders to protect the general public from harm caused by crime. The latter requires the CPL to protect the accused from improper prosecution and ensure that they are afforded all procedural rights in the criminal process.
>
> 2014, pp. 167–8

Others see this as a tension between the aspiration for a (socialist) rule of law and the limits of this aspiration under the political structures of socialism. Indeed, one of the enduring hallmarks of criminal justice reforms since the early 1980s has been their *aspirational* quality. Party-state authorities have publicly stated for decades that they aspire to developing a socialist rule of law. Since the PRC's first CPL in 1979, party authorities have aspired to build into the law broadly conceived due process protections. Deng declared that laws would need to be digested rapidly by a legally untrained judiciary, favoring what Ronald Keith calls a "fast-track" (1994, p. 20) approach to legal development. Deng's fast-tracking in the 1980s set in place a tendency by the party-state to make lofty announcements about justice system reform without the detailed procedural safeguards in place to deliver what was necessary to realize these systemic reforms in a way that guaranteed their enforceability. Procedural laws regulations were established, but mechanisms to enforce them effectively were not forthcoming.

Keith considers that this fast-track approach was summed up in Deng's dictum that "[some] law is better than no law, [and] faster [law-making] is better than slower [law-making]" (1994, p. 20). Here the idea was to advance a rule of law through the proxy of aspirational goal-making, rather than taking the slower and more politically fraught path of building into the system detailed and enforceable guarantees of due process. Establishing capacity to enforce procedural rules required inserting into the system legal remedies and legal liability for procedural misconduct. But this did not happen. Given the chaos of the Cultural Revolution, legislators focused on maintaining a sufficient degree of social stability conducive to economic modernization. This meant that they would need to keep the law sufficiently elastic to cope with any new and emerging threat to social stability. Legal elasticity meant that procedural protections were limited. Procedural due process guarantees to protect citizens' rights were not a focus of attention for those who drafted the 1979 CPL or for those involved in judicial practice. For both, the emphasis was on the political aspiration to guarantee social stability as a precondition to economic prosperity, which the party-state privileged above all goals.

Party authorities broadly defined social instability as something that runs counter to the smooth progress of modernization. Those who cause instability therefore need to be dealt with punitively. This understanding runs counter to assertions by legal scholars such as Tang Jinzong (2007) that strong laws that sustain due process are the ultimate safeguard against instability. On this nexus between social stability and law in 1990s Chinese jurisprudence, Keith and Lin observed that scholars argued then that meaningful and sustained development and enforcement of procedural law could work more effectively than anti-crime crackdowns to deal with the social fallout of a marketized economy. In the late 1990s, Chinese legal scholars reasoned along the lines that:

> The law becomes a handy and even rational tool by which to reinforce social stability on the basis of protecting rights and interests. Through its distributive and judicial justice, it is expected to provide an efficient basis for stability in the uncertain context of rapid economic change and related polarization of society.
>
> KEITH AND LIN 2001, p. 43

Chinese scholars have identified a crucial consequence of the failure of this alternative vision of procedural justice to flourish in China. It is the reluctance of legislators who aspired to a rule of law to build into the procedural law legal remedies for infringement of procedural rules. Rules against misconduct or mistakes are present in the law, but legal consequence and remedies for infringement of these rules are largely absent. Failure on the part of lawmakers to legislate on such infringement is the reason that the alternative vision of procedural justice has not developed within the politicolegal culture to provide this basis for stability. The leading Chinese legal scholar Chen Ruihua observes that because of this dearth of legal remedy China's criminal procedure has become a "malfunctioning system." He explains:

> The legal procedures established by the legislature are evaded or set aside in actual practice, such that the written regulations of the CPL are, to varying degrees, empty formulations.... To be sure the malfunctioning of the criminal process refers primarily to the fact that there is no way to effectively implement the procedures legally prescribed by the legislature.[8]
>
> 2011, p. 361

Chen's key point—and indeed the key to all debates about the CPL's lack of enforcement teeth—is that enforcement of procedural rules requires that the CPL set out legal liability and legal remedies to deter misconduct and to address procedural mistakes or improprieties. Under China's procedural law, "liability" for noncompliance with this law is limited to simply announcing that a certain action is "invalid" (2011, p. 361). As Chen explains:

> This means that the "principle that one bear liability for his own actions" as emphasized in substantive law, is not applied in procedural law. The agent of a procedural violation will not necessarily suffer a personal loss for the violation, but instead simply not enjoy the benefit he would have had without the violation.
>
> 2011, p. 363

Why does the lack of legal remedy and legal liability in the CPL remain a hallmark of the system today? A key reason concerns an issue that has framed scholarly discussion and debate on the CPL since the late 1990s. Keith and Lin articulated this issue in terms of a question that remains as pertinent today as it was for scholars in the 1990s: "Can procedural law act to support substantive law while remaining independently aloof from it?" (Keith and Lin, 2001, p. 43)

Scholars in both China and the West see that poor development of detailed and enforceable procedural rules in the CPL is the product of an overarching political mindset that recognizes checks and balances as a bulwark to, rather than beneficial for, guaranteeing social stability (Biddulph 2015; Biddulph et al. 2017a; Chen G 2007; Chen J 2016a; Chen R 2011, 2016; Chen and Yu 2014; Fu 2011; Guo 2014; Li Y 2014; Liang and He 2014; Liebman 2011; Ng and He 2017; Rosenzweig 2011, 2017; Rosenzweig et al. 2013; Sapio 2010). Scholars glean from various official pronouncements on criminal justice reform that social stability is construed as something that is best protected through coercive substantive

8 This view contrasts with rosier versions of China's legal achievements by, e.g., Wang L 2006.

law backed by minimal enforcement provisions. Rather than developing credible and consistent legal rules to resolve disputes and to mediate between disparate values and interests—institutional processes that members of society may grow to trust over time—the party-state's politicolegal policy has long reinforced a preference for prioritizing the political utility of substantive law over the legal utility of procedural law. Reforms to the criminal law process have therefore been circumscribed by these party authorities within the boundaries of what they consider conducive to preserving social stability, which they accept as a precondition for China's modernization and rejuvenation. Sapio et al. see this circumscription of procedural reform as a product of the way in which the party-state articulates "justice" as a general concept, that "individuals, society and the nation *ought to be given what they are due*" (2017, p. 10). They explain:

> In China, as a minimum common denominator, this notion [of justice] lies at the heart of party-state policy agendas, slogans and buzz-words. The party-state uses the popular understanding of "what is due" in articulating its role as provider of justice and protector of society from injustice and inequality in order to give the populace what is perceived as their due. It has sought to fulfil its protective role by striving for the goals of raising the people out of poverty; building a more inclusive society; achieving social harmony, a sustainable economic growth; and a development centered on the people, achieving and maintaining regional and global hegemony.
>
> SAPIO ET AL. 2017, pp. 10–11

An important question here is: who determines "what individuals, society and the nation are due"? The party-state "dominates and jealously guards the political space around which this dominant political logic about justice is based" (Sapio et al. 2017, p. 11) by promoting its notion of justice through political discourse. This includes not only broad discursive platforms such as the Harmonious Society, but also specific language that broadly correlates with notions of procedural and substantive justice. For instance, in the early 2000s, the party formulated its own terminology to describe the procedural—substantive justice nexus. Authorities declared that criminal justice functionaries must decide on a criminal case in a way that achieves both "positive social outcomes" (*lianghao de shehui xiaoguo* 良好的社会效果) and "positive legal outcomes" (*lianghao de falü xiaoguo* 良好的法律效果) (Trevaskes 2007; Yin 2011). Subsequent party crime-control policies have called for criminal justice decision-makers to achieve judicial justice in criminal trials by "unifying" (*tongyi* 统一) or "integrating" (*xiangjiehe* 相结合) these outcomes for the overall benefit of party governance platforms.

Guo Zhiyuan explains the significance of this unifying/integrating as it operates in specific decision-making spheres in the criminal justice system. Illustrating with a specific example, Guo points out that when police decide whether to grant a suspect a mental health assessment, they often take into consideration public reaction to the decision. Police weigh the potential impact of social instability caused by negative public opinion in a local community that calls for just deserts, especially when a violent crime has been committed.[9] She argues:

> assessment of the potential social outcome has played an important role in decision making and has sometimes even been a priority consideration when police, prosecutors and judges are determining whether to grant a mental examination. Considering the potential social effect involves balancing the protection of rights between the defendant and the victim.... Consideration of social effect also involves the general public's attitude toward professional evaluations of insanity. In major criminal cases, especially where the offender is not obviously insane or where multiple victims are involved and there is public anger at the offender, official agencies are subject to significant pressure from the public to punish the offender. This generally tends to discourage the agencies from requesting mental health assessments. The public's ignorance of mental illness coupled with the still prevalent philosophy of an "eye for [an] eye" in Chinese society make it difficult for police, prosecutors and judges to strike a balance between judicial fairness, public opinion and social stability.
>
> GUO 2014, pp. 171–2

Chinese scholars such as Guo Zhiyuan who have for years advocated for meaningful procedural reform argue that "positive legal outcomes"—through rules that protect procedural rights—produce positive social outcomes and not the other way around.

1.3 *Asserting the Importance of Stability to Define the Limits of Justice System Reform*

In the late 1990s and early 2000s, justice system reform plans associated with Jiang Zemin's *yifa zhiguo* platform continued to be tied directly to the party's

9 For analyses of public opinion and criminal justice, particularly the death penalty, see Belkin 2017; Fu 2016b; Jiang 2016; Miao 2013.

overall economic modernization program.[10] The nature of China's rapid economic growth through marketization depended on the willingness of party leaders to allow, initially at least, highly uneven economic development to enable the large-scale creation of wealth that, through later distribution, would eventually bring about a "moderately prosperous society" for the majority of citizens. The unprecedented rate of economic growth in the 1990s was facilitated by an approach to economic development through developing industries and enterprises that many around the world consider crony capitalism. The imperative for speed and the scale of development through marketization meant that this nationwide economic program was unimpeded by robust legal protections over labor and environment because strong oversight would have placed at risk the pace and scale of economic success (Trevaskes et al. 2014).[11]

But although this path to prosperity, in which the annual national economic growth rate was 8 to 10 percent, was successful in raw economic terms, it became increasingly apparent beginning in the late 1990s that it carried a high social and political cost. This development mode precipitated high social dissatisfaction, especially in areas where forced land acquisition were rampant, and where lax labor and environmental regulations were the norm (Fewsmith 2012; Lam 2009; Mattis 2012; Minzner 2013). Although the party-state had developed laws intended to regulate economic activities, the central authorities did not encourage their strict enforcement in subnational jurisdictions, where local government revenues depended on land sales and development (Biddulph 2015). Local governments had a vested interest in protecting privately owned as well as state-owned capital development. So, rather than strictly enforce regulations that might potentially slow down the momentum for economic growth and their own economic well-being, they allowed development to proceed in a socially and environmentally unsustainable way (van Rooij 2014). This situation enabled legally privileged state—and privately-owned enterprises to prosper at the expense of citizens, who lacked the capacity to protect themselves from the consequences of newly deregulated market forces.

The Sixteenth Party Congress Decision in 2002 acknowledged that, to enable the tasks of reform and development in China, the party would need to maintain a long-term, harmonious social environment (Lin 2004). The Party's Politico-Legal Commission in Beijing (China's main law and security policy

10 For insightful analyses of the general scholarship on *yifa zhiguo*, see Chen A 2016; Peerenboom 1999; Seppanen 2014, 2016, 2017; Wang C 2010; Zhu 2010.

11 For an insightful study of the connection between criminal law and economic development, see Lewis 2014.

organ) began to realign the country's justice and security policies to address three national tasks: enabling reform, encouraging development, and maintaining social stability (Lin 2004). These three agendas were cast as the drivers of the direction and timing of legal developments throughout the decade of the 2000s. They were linked ideologically to two main political programs—the Harmonious Society and Stability Maintenance—which the administration of Hu Jintao used to rationalize politicolegal policy and practice (Wang L 2007). Social stability became even more important as unprecedented rates of social protest accompanied growth in the gross domestic product. Social unrest, protests against injustice, and dissatisfaction with the unequal distribution of wealth brought about what the party deemed an increasingly unstable society (Chen 2012; Liebman 2011). A preoccupation with managing instability reshaped the party-state's approaches not only in handling civil disputes (Woo and Gallagher 2011) but also in the realm of criminal justice (Lam 2009; Liebman 2011; Mattis 2012; Minzner 2013; Ng and He 2016, 2017; Trevaskes 2009).

The party-state's disinclination or inability to ease tensions between the demands of breakneck economic growth and the requirements for lasting structural reform continued throughout the 2000s. The authorities were willing to accept some degree of social discord but would not allow social unrest to reach levels that would threaten China's prospects for a moderately prosperous society (Chen X 2012). Again, we find that in the realm of criminal justice the short-term imperative to contain social instability prevailed over alternative possibilities for change that could have set in place effective due process mechanisms to curb abuses of power. Short-term repression had a higher chance of success in terms of perpetuating one-party rule.

Several Chinese legal scholars at the time, such as Chen Guangzhong and Chen Weidong, argued for the development of more robust checks and balances within the criminal justice system, asserting that improving weak government and legal oversight mechanisms would enhance the prospects for long-term stability and prosperity (Chen G 2007; Chen W 2006). But the party leadership also recognized what it saw as an inherent difficulty in going all out to build structures for legal checks and balances to support institutional legitimacy. The authorities realized that institutionalizing system-wide procedural justice protections in the legal system would be the ultimate guarantee of long-term social stability. But they determined that building up and sustaining such a goal could not be realized in the short term because strict rule to enforce accountability might impede the desired scale and speed of economic growth. Instead, authorities stepped up the use of coercive measures to deal with crime, dissent, and instability. In the immediate post-Mao era, the rejection of class struggle colored the view of criminal justice, and China's criminal law was not depoliticized but, rather, was "repoliticized" (Trevaskes 2010) to ensure the stability imperative.

From 1983 to late 2003, *yanda* policy was employed in the form of anti-crime campaigns to deter and punish serious criminal activity (Bakken 2000; Dai 2010; Tanner H 1999; Tanner M 2000; Trevaskes 2007, 2010, 2012). This policy was effected in both everyday routine criminal justice decision-making and targeted periodic campaigns to combat serious and violent crimes. The pervasive implementation of *yanda* anti-crime policy over two decades was partly enabled by manipulation of wording in the CPL about what constitutes the standard of proof in a criminal case and by truncating trial and appeal processes in practice. Indeed, this policy is contemporary China's most notorious example of how substantive justice goals can so easily overshadow procedural justice concerns. Until the early 2000s, to deliver "severe and swift" justice against *yanda* targets, politicolegal authorities lowered the standard of proof needed to determine a defendant's culpability. "The two basics" (*liang ge jiben* 两个基本) became the standard of proof used to determine guilt in a *yanda*-targeted criminal case. To secure a conviction, judges needed only to be satisfied that the "basic" facts of a case were clear and that the "basic" evidence was sufficient (Trevaskes 2007, 2010, 2012). The success of *yanda* policy implementation was evaluated in terms of procuring "positive social outcomes" in the form of reduced crime incidence, which was seen as an indicator of a more stable social order.

Even in the 1990s, authorities in the party-state structure were well aware of the danger that the *yanda* approach presented for the burgeoning development of judicial legitimacy (Tanner 2005). Supreme People's Court (SPC) Chief Justice Xiao Yang argued at the time that the outcomes of criminal cases could truly be socially efficacious only when a proper standard of proof is met—that is, when "the facts of each case are clear and the evidence is reliable and sufficient" (*anjian shishi qingchu, zhengju queshi chongfen* 案件事实清楚 证据确实充分). In other words, court judgments could have positive social outcomes only if the procedures followed at trial to obtain the outcome were legally credible (Trevaskes 2007).

Beyond *yanda*, senior party leaders also had another concern. They were long aware of how the dynamics of the three moving parts of China's modernization—reform, development, and stability—would affect the building of accountability in the justice system. As Murray Scot Tanner (2013) has observed, in 2005 President Hu Jintao declared that, since China had reached a critical juncture on the road to modernity, preserving social stability was essential for maintaining the momentum of China's development and economic growth. Failure to do so would result in "economic stagnation and protracted social upheavals" (Hu, cited in Tanner 2013, p. 89). Tanner identifies three key assumptions of the party's economic modernization strategy at the time that help explain the problematic link between reform, development, and stability. The first is that sustained economic growth was the ultimate guarantee of social peace. The second is that economic growth in and of itself was insufficient to sustain the long-lasting legitimacy of the party-state. The party therefore needed to reform state institutions to enhance its capacity to govern.[12] It needed to adhere to the principles of due process by directly addressing the governance failures that were causing public protest and dissent. Ultimately, mechanisms for regulatory oversight and accountability needed to be made the bedrock of political and government legitimacy. The third assumption is that, despite acknowledging the imperative of meaningful accountability reforms, social instability still needed to be contained decisively in the prevailing environment of breakneck economic growth. Therefore, politicolegal authorities accepted that only by building rule of law through accountability reforms could the goals of sustained economic and social stability be fulfilled in the long run. But during the interim period of transition to the market, politicolegal crackdowns were still required to control the social fallout from economic reform (Tanner 2013).

After 2003, when policing priorities changed from *yanda* to Stability Maintenance and building a Harmonious Society (Trevaskes 2010, 2012), criminal justice reformers began to see the value of tempering harsh justice with lenient punishment to help maintain stability. Party authorities sought to deliver substantive justice reforms, which both promoted and reflected the success of the two new governance platforms. Nowhere is this trend more evident than in the Harmonious Society—era policy called Balancing Leniency and Severity (*kuanyan xiangi* 宽严相济) (Dai 2010; Trevaskes 2010, 2012). By the end of 2006, this was declared China's new foundational criminal justice policy, which SPC reformers used to push for reforms in China's death penalty system (Johnson and Zimring 2009; Trevaskes 2010, 2012). These death penalty reforms vastly improved procedural justice provisions through SPC regulations and through an amendment to the Organic Law of the People's Court in 2007, which changed the authority for final review and approval of executions from the provincial to the central level. In many ways, these death penalty reforms were the most marked advancements in China's criminal justice system for decades.

---

12 For an examination of the the integration of the party and the state in China including the bifurcation of state decision-making processes and the cohabitation of the two normative systems of party and state, see Li 2015.

At the minor crime end of the spectrum was "harmonious justice" (*hexie sifa* 和谐司法). This entailed a new system of criminal reconciliation (*xingshi hejie* 刑事和解) (Ng and He 2016, 2017; Shi 2008; Trevaskes 2009) initiated before or during the trial process, to bypass the need for a full trial in cases of minor assaults and traffic accidents. It also translated into a sustained effort to target lenient sentencing for minor assaults, traffic accidents, and other minor crimes (Liebman 2015) and to truncate the trial process for very minor offenses (Biddulph 2015, 2016, 2017; Biddulph et al. 2017a). At the serious crime end of the spectrum, harmonious justice translated into what authorities called "criminal mediation" (*xingshi tiaojie* 刑事调解), an approach to capital sentencing in which judges negotiated with a murder victim's family to obtain their acceptance of a suspended death sentence, in exchange for the defendant's expression of remorse and payment of civil compensation to the victim's family, the amound of which is negotiated between the perpetrator's and victim's families. In exchange, the victim's family would agree not to protest the downgrading of the defendant's sentence from immediate execution to a suspended death sentence (a sentence which is downgraded to a life sentence after two years); such protests could cause social instability (Johnson and Zimring 2009; Ng and He 2016; Trevaskes 2012).

By 2008, party authorities had begun to acknowledge more openly the potentially destabilizing effects of their own social stability initiatives. At this stage, they had no intention of reforming stability maintenance practices, such as aggressive mediation (Fu 2013), but the instability problem had precipitated attempts to approach reform of the criminal justice system in a new way that would support stability maintenance operations while, at the same time, attempting to improve oversight mechanisms for the criminal justice system. It was apparent by 2008 that stronger party input from Beijing to offset corruption and interference in local court matters was imperative to address what had become an explosive social stability problem. The Politburo recognized that systemic entrenchment of power relations made the development of accountability building through CPL reform a difficult task. Central party authorities therefore used their political imprimatur to oversee a 2008 plan for justice system reform. This plan aimed to improve the prospects for procedural and substantive justice, recognizing that the party's own Stability Maintenance and Harmonious Society initiatives had seriously damaged the public credibility of judicial institutions (*People's Daily* 2008; Trevaskes 2011).

The Politburo recognized that enhancing credibility and institutional authority would require a complex mix of reforms to deal with the structural deficiencies at the local level. Court agencies were beholden to local governments because for decades their income had relied on local sources. This meant that, at each subnational or local level (county, municipal, province), courts could be influenced by local government officials who might seek to interfere in locally sensitive cases. According to the 2008 Politiburo document, improvements in judicial justice would be achieved by strengthening the oversight (supervision) functions of key political and politicolegal actors: procuratorates overseeing court decisions and people's congresses overseeing court and procuratorates at the local level, along with superior courts and superior party committees overseeing their subordinate agencies (Trevaskes 2011).

The general intentions of the plan for system-wide reform of criminal justice were announced publicly in the *People's Daily* (2008), but specific details about the 60 reform provisions in the document were withheld from the public. The party's 2008 plans for justice system reform centered on improving judicial justice and efficiency. Among other initiatives, it included the intention to return the funding of courts from local jurisdictions to central authorities in Beijing and to strengthen the supervisory oversight powers of the procuratorate.[13] Although some of the substantive justice reform plans for criminal sentencing, such as through the policy of Balancing Severity and Leniency in criminal sentencing, were successfully implemented through various "leniency" initiatives (Liebman 2015), propriety and oversight goals, such as shifting court budgetary funding to the central government, were not. These reform intentions were announced in a year when the political winds had shifted decisively to a more conspicuous emphasis on party leadership. "Politics in command" overtones were present, not only in this party plan but also in the wider political realm, as signaled by the appointment of the political conservative Wang Shengjun to the SPC and the issuing of the "Three Supremes" policy (one supreme being the leadership of the party).

Waiting in the wings for nearly a decade was the amendment of the CPL that had been redrafted a number of times over the years. The CPL was first amended in 1996 to fill the gaps in the 1979 CPL by promoting an adversarial-style trial, but it remained what Lewis identified as an inquisitorial system in "adversarial clothing" (2011, p. 652). The party's obsession with stability maintenance throughout the 2000s stalled CPL reform until the law was finally amended in 2012. Leading procedural scholars, including Song Yinghui, Fan Chongyi, Chen Weidong, Guo Zhiyuan, and Zuo Weimin, had highlighted numerous flaws in the 1996 CPL[14] and participated in pilot programs across the country throughout the 2000s. These programs experimented with various

13 For an examination of the problem of local government funding local courts, see He 2009; Ng and He 2017.

14 For an examination of the flaws of the CPL, see Chen 2011.

new CPL initiatives, ranging from criminal reconciliation and other special measures to new draft provisions, such as making compulsory the system of audio recording criminal interrogations.[15] The Party's 2008 plan was at least successful in getting CPL reform back on the legislative agenda, culminating in the promulgation of an amended CPL in 2012, a document that some Chinese scholars clearly considered a political and institutional compromise among different interests and actors (Guo 2014).[16]

1.4 *Reasserting Central Party Power to Improve and Standardize Criminal Trial Outcomes*

As observed above, scholars in China and the West see that the Hu Jintao era of criminal justice reform focused on substantive justice defined broadly in relation to the Harmonious Society—Stability Maintenance agendas. In contrast, the rhetorical focus in the Xi Jinping era is on proceduralism and building accountability through strong and centralized party control (Brødsgaard and Grünberg 2014; Chen J 2016b; Clarke 2015; deLisle 2017; He 2018; Li A 2016; Li L 2015; Peerenboom 2015). Immediately after their ascendence to power, the new party leadership, headed by President Xi, began to make rhetorical noises about changing the party-state's response to social instability, retreating from Hu-era Harmonious Society—Stability Maintenance discourse. The new leadership began realigning the country's politicolegal agenda by gradually withdrawing its hard stance on stability maintenance, which was eroding public confidence in the law, and returning to a rhetorical emphasis on *yifa zhiguo*.

Loss of public trust in the capacity of politicolegal authorities to fairly apply the law was central in this retreat. The new party leadership quickly began to realign the politicolegal agenda promoting *yifa zhiguo* rhetoric. In late 2012 and early 2013, an immediate upsurge in party references to the rule of law signaled intentions within the party to move decisively to rebalance power relations within and among the judicial and security organs to make them more conducive to "supervision" and "mutual restraint" and, ultimately, to long-term regime resilience. Politicolegal authorities, particularly senior SPC judges, such as SPC Deputy President Shen Deyong, began to extol the virtues of the rule of law and procedural justice, highlighting the SPC and party's intention to extend *yifa zhiguo* with lasting solutions to the complex problems of

15 For an example of the various pilot programs, see Guo 2011; Liu and Wang 2015. See also Part 3 in this article.

16 For an examination of the details of the CPL, see Chen J 2013, 2016a; Li Y 2014. For a critique of the 2012 CPL, see Rosenzweig et al. 2013.

interference, corruption, and other disruptive issues, along with the intention to standardize decision-making across the country (China Radio International 2012; Shen 2015).

Overall, the focus at this time was on fostering stronger oversight of political and judicial authorities at the local level (Chen J 2016a; Zhang 2016). In November 2012, Xi and senior politicolegal authorities began to promote a renewed commitment to proceduralism with promises of transparency and preventing miscarriages of justice. SPC judges and legal commentators immediately began to hold open discussions about the nature of judicial justice. For instance, in November 2012, Shen Deyong joined a number of leading Chinese legal scholars in an online forum in which he stated that to reorient the country's judiciary toward more effective and credible decision-making, "we need first to establish the correct concept of justice ... second, to establish institutional mechanisms to ensure the strict application of procedural law, to further promote the concept of procedural justice ... and third ... to improve the individual quality of judges" (China Radio International 2012).

Judicial justice, Shen asserted, "is related to the construction of the democratic rule of law, to *yifa zhiguo*, and to the realization of social fairness and justice," but judicial decision-making in the PRC is still not sufficiently "standardized" (China Radio International 2012). In 2013, the SPC called for various measures to standardize judicial decision-making to enhance the credibility (*gongxinli* 公信力) of local courts (SPC 2013), relating their lack of credibility to regular miscarriages of justice. To this end, various organs, including the party's Politico-Legal Commission and the Ministry of Public Security (MPS) issued regulations on preventing miscarriages of justice that explicitly called for improving the process of reviewing evidence in criminal trials in strict accordance with the provisions set out in the amended 2012 CPL (MPS 2013; CPLC 2013). The Party Central Politico-Legal Commission Opinion on Preventing Miscarriages of Justice circulated in 2013 (CPC 2013) requires judges to exclude evidence obtained through torture or other illegal means and to use only evidence presented in court as the basis for conviction. A few months after releasing this Opinion, the SPC released its provisions on Preventing Miscarriages of Justice, which reaffirmed the ground rules for protection of due process (Biddulph et al. 2017a; Nesossi 2017; Trevaskes and Nesossi 2014). The party began to promote the prevention of miscarriages of justice as a hallmark of Xi's renewed push for proceduralism. Officials articulated a particular political line that upholds the idea of the party-state's protective role in preventing injustices. Nesossi (2017) sees these moves as an attempt to dominate the political environment in which the political logic of redressing and preventing miscarriages of justice is discussed.

On November 12, 2013, the party announced a swath of economic, governance, and judicial reform intentions in the highly anticipated Decision of the third plenum of the eighteenth party congress. The Decision declared that several measures would be taken to strengthen China's justice system and ultimately its socialist rule of law. The rule of law envisaged in this document would not limit the role of the party in justice affairs but would sustain the party's role so as to instill fairer outcomes through stricter party and institutional oversight (Biddulph et al. 2017a; Chen J 2016b; Zhang 2016). Building credibility into the system would therefore necessitate making the promotion of transparency, procedural justice, and prevention of miscarriages of justice a centerpiece of Xi-era legitimacy discourse (Daum 2014; Nesossi 2016, 2017; Xi 2015; Zhao 2017).

The third and fourth plenums of the eighteenth party congress produced reform decisions that included some of the unsuccessful 2008 party plan initiatives mentioned above. As in discussion of them in the 2008 party plan, the initiatives were cast as "optimizing the allocation of justice system authority" (*youhua sifa zhiquan peizhi* 优化司法职权配置). This is an umbrella concept that refers to various means of rebalancing the scales of power to effect a fairer justice system and to protect against both the negative fallout of judicial corruption and the localization of justice that came about in the Hu era (Li S 2016). Examples of optimizing this authority include the decision to transfer budgetary authority over local courts from the local/subprovincial government to the provincial level (Chen J 2016b; Zhang 2016); moves to clarify the responsibility of judges in cases at each level of the judiciary (SPC Monitor 2017); and the effort to reduce the power of internal adjudication committees. These committees in each court comprise senior court officials who are not present at trial but nevertheless recommend trial decisions relating to criminal culpability and sentencing in difficult or complex criminal trials (He 2012; Li L 2014). This reform was to deregulate (Zhang 2016) the supervision of courtroom decision-making by senior court staff via the court's adjudication committee, while improving judicial transparency and the independence of trial judges (Chen J 2016a; SPC Monitor 2016; Zhang 2016).

Xi-era *yifa zhiguo* narrative-building began in earnest after the shutdown of the liberal constitutionalism debate in 2013.[17] By late 2013, it had become clear that the leadership under Xi intended to rebalance the accountability–coercion equation. But, rather than reducing coercive crackdowns while increasing accountability, the Xi leadership decided to intensify both. Synchronous with the accountability reforms discussed earlier, the Xi leadership

17 For a discussion of the constitutionalism debate, see Creemers 2015.

rationalized the intensified use of crackdowns and campaigns against oppositional elements in society, including human rights lawyers who continued to openly contest the party's monopoly over public discussion about the form that accountability and procedural justice should take in Chinese society. The party would deal head on with the fallout from decades of corruption and the ever-increasing social dissent that it produced by further centralizing party control. This dual intensification of accountability and coercive measures was framed as part of Xi's *yifa zhiguo* platform. In late 2013 the party began to reassert its legitimacy claims through *yifa zhiguo* propaganda, which stressed both accountability reforms and coercive "dictatorship" measures against the people's enemies under the overall ideological rubric of the *yifa zhiguo* platform, which itself comes under the party's leadership. The Xi administration's plans aimed to further embed what authorities saw as legitimate party leadership over all aspects of the justice system, while, at the same time, discouraging illegitimate interference in specific court cases by local party and government officials (Li L 2016; Zhao 2017). Hence, senior party calls to respect judicial independence did not infer that the party was pulling away from its overall leadership over the judiciary, nor was it in any way inferring a push to more Westernized understanding of judicial independence (Liu 2017).

1.5 *Procedural Justice Discourse and Scholarship in the Xi Era*

After 2014, Harmonious Society and Stability Maintenance were shunted from the party political landscape and therefore from the dominant political narrative. Now scholarly circles saw a resurgence in *yifa zhiguo* discourse in line with its elevation in party propaganda. For instance, China's premier law journal, *Legal Science* (*Faxue* 法学), until then assumed by most in the field to be a relatively independent journal, clearly demonstrated the pervasiveness of Xi's *yifa zhiguo* discourse in the academic literature at the highest levels of Chinese legal scholarship. Its July 2016 issue was devoted to Xi and *yifa zhiguo*, with articles such as:

- On the New Thinking and Strategy behind Xi Jinping's Comprehensive "Governing the Nation in Accordance with the Law"
- The Shape and Characteristics of Xi Jinping's "Governing the Nation in Accordance with the Law" Thinking
- Perfecting the Idea of Making "Governing the Constitution in Accordance with the Law" the Core Tenet of the Legal System with Chinese Characteristics
- Analysis of Xi Jinping's Route to the Rule of Law
- Contemplations and Explorations of Xi Jinping's Establishment of the Rule of Law Relating to National Security and the Military
- Research on Xi Jinping's "Rule of Law in Xinjiang"

– On the Stabilization of the Law and Rule of (Civil) Law: Xi Jinping's Rule of Law Idea and Its Manifestation in All Areas of the Law.

Today, a considerable number of scholars in China encourage the idea of procedural justice as an important part of Xi's *yifa zhiguo* program, promoting party discourse, such as "procedural justice is the prerequisite for judicial justice" and is its "last line of defense" (Li L 2015). Yet other procedural law scholars are more circumspect, arguing that the entire political culture of criminal justice needs to be changed before legal reforms can be effective in bringing about meaningful procedural justice reform. They describe the prevailing political culture of criminal procedure as continuing to embody an ethos of "investigation centrism" (*zhencha zhongxin zhuyi* 侦查中心主义) (Chen R 2016, 2017; Chen W 2016a, 2016b; Shan 2016). This catch-phrase encapsulates a strong inclination in the justice system to downplay the importance of rigorously testing testimony and material evidence through cross-examination at trial. In the absence of such cross-examination challenging the police and prosecution's evidence, it is easier for judges to accept the written testimony as established "fact."

Political pronouncements about the importance of judicial justice and *yifa zhiguo* are not new and harken back to the early period of reforms in the 1990s. What is new is the degree to which the idea of proceduralism has come to play a defining role in Xi's overall *yifa zhiguo* governance platform. As noted above, the rhetorical centerpiece of Xi's reform drive is the 2014 Decision of the fourth plenum of the eighteenth party congress, which, along with the third plenum Decision a year earlier, set out the master plan for due process reforms. One such fourth plenum reform initiative is "placing the trial at the center of criminal proceedings" (*yishenpan weizhongxin* 以审判为中心), referred to as "trial centeredness." This is based on the idea that it is the criminal trial, not the criminal investigation, that should be where decisions about guilt and culpability are made (Biddulph et al. 2017a). The 2014 fourth plenum Decision instructs on the imperative of trial centeredness:

> Promote structural reform in litigation with trials at the center and ensure that the facts and evidence of cases under investigation, examination, and prosecution can stand the test of law. Fully implement evidentiary judgment rules; collect, fix, preserve, investigate, and use evidence strictly according to the law; perfect systems for witnesses and experts appearing in court; and ensure that courtroom hearings play a decisive role in ascertaining the facts, identifying the evidence, protecting the right of action, and adjudicating impartially.
>
> CCP CENTRAL COMMITTEE 2014

After the fourth plenum in late 2014, efforts were made to develop trial centeredness into a catch-all doctrine of criminal procedural justice employed at the highest levels of power to implore police and prosecutors to adopt three central concepts: the criminal trial is the only place in which criminal culpability should be determined; guilt can be determined only by establishing the facts of the case through rigorous testing in court, not merely by presentation of written testimony in the case file; and the evidence presented in court must be obtained legally (Chen et al. 2016; Chen and Zhou 2016; Shen 2015; Zhang and Cao 2017). Xi's Central Leading Group confirmed the importance of trial centeredness in 2016, drafting a 21-article Opinion on the central ingredients of trial centeredness issued that year under the joint authority of the SPC, the Supreme People's Procuratorate, the Ministry of Public Security, the Ministry of State Security, and the Ministry of Justice (Joint Opinion 2016; Shan 2016). This Opinion promotes the idea of procedural fairness (Shan 2016; *Zhongguo ribao* 2017). It largely comprises provisions already set out in the 2012 CPL and other regulations (Zhou 2016), but here it is collected in one document for the first time and under Xi's direct imprimatur. The SPC followed up in February 2017 with specific provisions, including a new process of using the pretrial conference for evaluating interrogational torture claims (Daum 2017; SPC 2017).[18]

2 The Policy-Implementing Structures of the Criminal Process

2.1 *Crime Control and Due Process*

What do scholars see as the role played by the existing structures of criminal justice in the discussion above? Western philosophical canons on procedural justice, such as John Rawls's *A Theory of Justice* have been the subject of lively debate in Chinese scholarship (Seppanen 2014, 2016, 2017). But these discussions revolve around broadly defined procedural ideals, not legal structure. Furthermore, Rawlsian justice tends to sit uncomfortably with Chinese criminal procedural justice debates because it speaks about justice as it should operate in a liberal democracy. Most Chinese scholars of criminal procedural justice, particularly critical legal scholars, axiomatically begin their analysis with an assumption that the criminal justice system and its processes operate in a particular political system that sets the ideological boundaries for its development (Seppanen 2014).[19]

18 See Part 3 of this article.

19 As Seppanen claims in relation to Chinese avant-garde legal scholars, "the assumption that there is no single, universally valid ideological blueprint for economic and social

In contrast to liberal democratic settings, in China most scholarship on criminal procedural justice concerns purpose and direction—that is, how procedural justice, and, by association, the fair trial, operate so as to advance the cause of socialist modernization. Although this is a truism acknowledged almost universally in the field in China, diverse approaches have been developed for articulating legal development and its relationship to socialist modernization. Some of them involve an assumption about the nature of legal development—that law in China advances from the party-state's relatively greater reliance on coercion until a threshold is reached at which mechanisms with relatively greater accountability override the need for the dominance of coercion. Scholarship in the general field of Chinese law sometimes articulates this as moving from no rule of law to gradual development of a "thin" rule of law (Peerenboom 1999) or from a model of law based on the dominant ideology in Mao's time to one based on pragmatism in the post-Mao era (Lo 1995; Yu 1989). Others in the specific field of criminal procedure law define this as a tension between crime control and due process models of criminal justice.

In the late 1990s, Chinese legal scholars began to talk about China's criminal justice process in terms of Herbert Packer's (1968) crime control and due process goals, seeing these goals as competing ideal-type models. Scholars such as Zuo Weimin and Song Yinghui (cited in Keith and Lin 2011, p. 184) described the crime control—due process nexus in terms of tension that needs to be balanced by provisions in the CPL. Legal academics who played a defining role in the early stage of the decade-long redrafting of the CPL in the 2000s were sensitive to the need to carefully craft their assertions for change by using the language of established official discourse. For instance, over a decade ago, the prominent legal scholar Chen Weidong advocated for legislative reform to the CPL by suggesting a mindset change "from the traditional view of emphasizing fighting [crime] and neglecting protection [of human rights] to a view that integrates the crime control imperative with human rights protection" (2006, p. 154); "moving from a view that emphasizes substantive justice to one that emphasizes procedural justice" (2006, p. 155); and moving from emphasizing both judicial justice and efficiency to stressing judicial justice "with due consideration [given] to efficiency" (2006, p. 158).

In contrast, Guo Zhiyuan's work tries to avoid a teleological approach, seeing that, despite "progression" and "improvement," due process provisions in the 2012 CPL continue to be functional for crime control and stability maintenance.

---

development needs … to be qualified with the recognition of contextual political and ideological conflicts and the pre-eminence of hegemonic ideological structures" (2014, p. 124).

Rather than seeing crime control and due process as relatively discrete models or goals, she sees one as functional for the other. For instance, in relation to new 2012 CPL provisions—the exclusionary rules protecting against interrogational torture, compulsory measures, and investigative measures that enhance crime control—she says:

> One could argue that all the anti-torture mechanisms will help to strengthen human rights protections by imposing more limitations on government organizations that have contributed to rights abuses. However, the ultimate purpose of these measures is to prevent wrongful convictions. The same is true of measures to prevent coercive confession since this not only impairs procedural fairness, but also and more importantly leads to wrongful convictions. Given that Chinese society has exhibited increasingly lower tolerance of wrongful convictions, the Chinese legislature had no choice but to release a set of measures to eliminate interrogational torture, or at least reduce it to a minimum. The amendments to the compulsory measures and investigative measures ... clearly indicate their designers' intention to enhance the capacity for punishing crimes, the purpose of which is to maintain the stability of society. For example, residential surveillance (RS), especially in a designated place, was conceived mainly to control suspects chargeable with financial crimes. And according to some commentators, the legislature also hopes to replace the practice of "double designation" (*shuanggui, shuangzhi*) with RS in a designated place. Financial and corruption crimes threaten social stability, and improvements to RS are expected to help restore social order by punishing these crimes effectively.[20]
>
> GUO 2014, pp. 169–70

Here Guo makes the important point that criminal procedure reforms in the law are beneficial for enhancing institutional legitimacy and crime control. Legislators do not advance due process provisions as discrete legal principles independent from the overall goal of advancing socialist modernization. This line of reasoning can be taken one step further. We recall, earlier in this paper, Keith and Lin's question "Can procedural law act to support substantive law while remaining independently aloof from it?" (2001, p. 43). Chen Ruihua's work outlining the dysfunctional nature of the CPL suggests that, as long as the system of enforcement is weak, the law cannot remain aloof. His work

20 Note that *shuanggui* has been replaced by *liuzhi* 留置 (a codified form of custody) under the Supervision Law passed in March 2018.

and Guo's fit with what scholars in the general field of criminal law outside China have observed. In relation to the common law system, Bottomley and Bronitt argue that due process and crime control are not independent principles because "each is comprised by the competing demands of the other" (2011, p. 228). Therefore, they point to what Doreen McBarnett identifies as the false distinction that criminologists have often made about due process and crime control dichotomy (McBarnett, cited in Bottomley and Bronitt 2011, p. 228). McBarnett argues in relation to the British system:

> If the practice of criminal justice does not live up to its rhetoric one should not look only to the interactions and negotiations of those who put the law into practice but to the law itself. One should not look just to how the rhetoric of justice is subverted intentionally or otherwise by policemen bending the rules, by lawyers negotiating adversariness out of existence, by out-of-touch lawyers, judges or biased magistrates: one must also look at how it is subverted in the law. Police and court officials need not abuse the law to subvert the principles of justice; they need only use it. Deviation from the rhetoric of legality and justice is institutionalized in the law itself.
>
> MCBARNETT 1981, pp. 155–56

The key point here is that the law embodies and sustains the crime control goal and thus potentially (or in practice) delimits the development of procedural justice. Applying this observation to the Chinese context, how does the scholarly field see China's crime control model of justice institutionalized in the structures of the law?

2.2 *The Structures of Procedure in an Activist State*

In the late 1990s, Western scholars began to focus more directly on the political structures of power that shape Chinese criminal process, advancing the argument that legal structures need to be conceptualized, first and foremost, in relation to the context of state-building and governance (Findlay 1999; Jayasuriya 1999a, 1999b). In direct contrast to work that assumes a teleological link between economic development and liberalism, scholars such as Kanishka Jayasuriya have examined the structure of China's criminal process as an outcome of a particular "activist" disposition of the Chinese party-state.

Jayasuriya begins his discussion with an important distinction between the liberal conception of state power and what he calls the "statist" conception of state power. In the East Asian context, the predominance of statist state power has meant that the concept of the rule of law has been developed as a condition for state legitimation and rationalization, rather than as a "natural" consequence of economic development, as it occurred in Western economic environments. To this extent, in the East Asian region, law has been historically employed as a means of managing and regulating society. As he notes:

> It can be argued that the trajectory of state formation in East Asia has served to induce a curious twist to the Weberian model of legal rationality … instead of legal rationality being the outcome of a process of historical evolution, it becomes a set of routines and practices that underpin the colonial and the post-colonial states; and what is more, it is utilized to expand or entrench its power. Consequently, the techniques and routines of legal rationality are disconnected from their moorings in civil society, and attach themselves as instruments of state power.
>
> JAYASURIYA 1999b, p. 179

Since the law has been developed as part of the managerial and regulatory agendas of state development and state building, the form and content of the activities of legal institutions in this statist model of state power reflect the same managerial and regulatory goals of the state (Jayasuriya 1999b, pp. 179–80). In this context, the judicial—executive relationship is conceived as a form of "corporatism": a structure of state power that promotes "a certain conception of the good and implies a highly managed and regulated civil society, organically linked to the state" (1999b, pp. 198–99). Jayasuriya refers to "corporatism" in two respects:

> In one sense, it is used to denote the close consultation and collaboration between the executive and the judiciary—a form of concertation … In another sense, corporatism is used to identify a form of ideology, and particularly to underscore the role of organic conceptions of state and society that weave through nearly all corporatist discourses.
>
> 1999b, pp. 182–83

Through this framework, the judicial—executive relationship in the PRC can be conceived as a form of "corporatism" characterized by "a division of power rather than a separation of power"; close consultation between the judiciary and other executive agencies; a "strong tendency for the judiciary to yield to other agencies where these agencies are thought to have greater competence," and a strong tendency of the corporatist elements of judicial—executive relations to "draw sustenance from organic conceptions of the state" (1999b, pp. 198–99).

Jayasuriya's work is informed by the comparative law typology of Mirjan Damaška in *The Faces of Justice and State Authority* (1986). Damaška offers a typology of different types of modern legal systems based on the idea that a strong connection exists between the goals of the broader political culture and the system of justice administration. He explores the character of judicial authority and the functional attributes of justice administration as a way of comparing characteristics of legal processes. On the assumption of a link between the general character of political authority and the character of procedural design, he argues that a number of characteristics common to systems of justice administration are marked primarily by a hierarchically organized system of judicial authority. He contrasts these characteristics with what he calls "coordinated systems of judicial authority," which feature a less integrated, more horizontal distribution of authority (e.g., common law systems, which rely on lay officials, party control over proceedings, oral testimony, and limited review) (Damaška 1986).

In referring to how the broad goals or purposes of government are understood in each model and how they affect the format and characteristics of the judicial structure and the criminal process, Damaška posits two competing ideal-type models of the state: the reactive state and the activist state. He explains the reactive state as an ideal type of minimalist governance "limited to providing a supportive framework" that enables individuals in the state to pursue their own goals (Damaška 1986, p. 73). In the activist state, he sees that the functions of government are tailored to an interventionist pursuit of social goals, and the law is programmatic to the extent that it functions to realize policy goals of government (Damaška 1986, p. 82). The activist state "espouses or strives toward a comprehensive theory of the good life and tries to use it as a basis for a conceptually all-encompassing program of material and moral betterment of its citizens" (Damaška 1986, p. 80). In an activist state, law is an instrument for implementing and realizing state policy, so the judicial format in judicial institutions reflects a "policy-implementing" disposition. In contrast to the reactivist state's "conflict-resolving" disposition, in an activist state, the law "springs from the state and expresses its policies" (Damaška 1986, pp. 82, 147–80). Scholars including Capowski (2012), Nesossi (2012), and Trevaskes (2007) have found Damaška's typology a useful analytical tool in their explorations of Chinese law.

China's system of justice is akin to a continental inquisitorial system of law.[21] The hierarchical forms of authority characteristic of inquisitorial systems

---

21 For a description of China's procedural system as an inquisitorial system, see Capowski 2012; Yi 2012.

have a permanent career bureaucracy whose members perform duties in specialized stages controlled by strict adherence to technical and bureaucratic standards. Justice administration in hierarchical systems relies mainly on written records of proceedings and testimony, usually organized in case files that follow the case up the procedural ladder (Damaška 1986). Adversarial dispute resolution is not characteristic of the procedural format in this model, and the criminal trial is not a contest between equal parties; rather, it is organized essentially as an investigation, an inquiry in which fact finding is dominated by the case file system. In this model of criminal process, to a greater or lesser degree, the trial is a matter of tailoring the outcome of a dispute to fit the contours of existing government policies and procedural law acts as the handmaiden of substantive law, because trial decisions are legitimated primarily in terms of the correct outcomes that they embody. Thus a proper procedure "is one that increases the probability—or maximizes the likelihood—of achieving a substantively accurate result rather than one that successfully effects notions of fairness or protects some collateral substantive value" (Damaška 1986, pp. 147–48).

As noted earlier, Chinese party leaders have long argued that the structure of the criminal process needs to reflect basic fairness principles that protect the people's interests as a whole. Fairness principles are therefore part of the overall guiding ideology of the party, which delimits criminal procedural reform based on the notion that the party's interests manifest those of the people. Unsurprisingly, therefore, China's CPL closely aligns with two key characteristics of Damaška's policy-implementing ideal type. The first is the idea that the trial is essentially an inquiry, with the object of the inquiry (the defendant) as primarily a supplier of information. The second is that trial decisions are legitimated through a standard of proof that supports achieving an accurate result—interpreted as "accurate" to the extent that it fulfills the objectives of the CPL, including Article 1, which as noted earlier, states that the CPL's purpose is "to ensure correct enforcement of the Criminal Law, punish crimes, protect the people, protect national security and public security, and maintain the order of socialist society." Various procedural aspects support these policy-implementing goals. For example, the judge is not a "neutral listener" or "host" but a fact-finder (Bian and Li 2006, p. 167), working with "facts" that, more often than not, have already been "found" for the judge by police and prosecutors. These facts are presented to the court in the police file via the prosecution and are gathered in a case file that the judge is permitted to view before the trial (Chen R 2016, 2017).

2.3 *Mutual Coordination*

Over three decades ago, scholars such as Baum (1986) and Leng and Chiu (1985) pointed out that the characteristics of China's policy-implementing criminal process indeed align closely with the established relationship between the police, the procuratorate, and the courts in China as defined in its constitution. Scholars frequently refer to this relationship as the "iron triangle."[22] Article 135 of the 1982 Constitution states that, in handling criminal cases, the three organs "shall divide their functions, each taking responsibility for its own work," but that they must "coordinate their efforts and check each other to ensure the correct and effective enforcement of the law." The CPL refers to this as "mutual coordination and mutual restraint" (*huxiang peihe, huxiang zhiyue* 互相配合, 互相制约). As Zuo Weimin (2016) explains, this system of mutual coordination and mutual restraint represents the three links of a chain, with "work processes" differentiated by the three main stages: investigation, prosecution, and adjudication. Mutual restraint is provided in the supervisory role of the people's procuratorate over the court at the corresponding level; apart from the right to protest judgments made by people's courts, the procuratorate is also responsible for monitoring the legality of judgments and procedural decisions by the courts (Mou 2017b).

The promotion of mutual coordination and mutual restraint is a particularly apposite example of how authorities, from the start of the reform era in 1979, set up checks and balances in the law in a way that gives a general nod to ideas such as accountability and due process but not to the structures and legal provisions that guarantee their enforcement. An example is the principle of "supervision" as an expression of procedural propriety and mutual restraint. Zuo Weimin explains the logic in terms of the procuratorate's dual role in the CPL as prosecutor and chief "supervisor" over the criminal process. He notes that, if the procuratorate finds a violation of the law in the execution of a judgment, he/she can give notice to the executing organs to correct the violation. However, the procuratorate not only has supervisory power but also is the state's sole prosecution authority and therefore has a vested interest in gaining a conviction in a criminal case (Zuo 2016, 2017). It is not surprising that research on the causes of miscarriages of justice in China focus on "mutual restraint" mechanisms that are particularly weak, allowing evidence collected illegally at the investigation stage to move through the system undetected (Chen and Yu 2014; He 2016; He and He 2012; Jiang 2013, 2016; Nesossi 2017; Yang 2016).

The deficiencies of "mutual restraint" are present and clear in Chen Ruihua's work on procedural law. Earlier in this paper we noted that Chen describes

22 See, e.g., Jiang 2013; Liu and Halliday 2011, 2016.

China's criminal procedure as malfunctioning because of its dearth of legal remedies and lack of legal liability to address abuses of power, procedural mistakes, or improprieties that occur in the criminal process. He says that in place of detailed and enforceable remedy mechanisms is a system of "latent" regulations that are not officially broadcast as "regulations" per se but nevertheless operate as such. The latent regulations he lists as operating in criminal justice decision-making are highly generalized and amorphous. Though Chen's 2011 study was published before the 2012 CPL amendment, these problems largely remain today.

- Instead of the collegial panel, courts frequently promote the "presiding judge system."
- Instead of the principle of a "suspected crime is no crime", courts almost universally enforce such flexible methods as "a suspected crime gets a lighter punishment" or "send the case back to the other organs for additional investigation."
- Since it is impossible to implement the principle that a defendant's confession should be voluntary, there is, in practice, the notion that "those who exercise their defense rights should be punished more severely." Moreover, courts often take the defendant's not admitting one's guilt as a basis for increasing the sentence. This shows that defendants may be punished more heavily if they exercise their right to defense.
- The court rarely notifies witnesses, experts, and victims to testify in court. Instead, a norm has developed where witnesses, experts, and victims simply submit written testimony. The 'trial' consists mainly of the court reading out the dossier and records.
- Initially intended as a compulsory measure to ensure the smooth operation of the criminal process, arrest should be both temporary and done according to procedure. But in judicial practice, it has commonly become a precondition to conviction and prediction of punishment.
- Bail initially served as a substitute for indefinite detention, or to reduce the use of [pre-trial] detention. But the public security bureau and procuratorate commonly use it to deal with minor criminal cases, or, in cases where the evidence is weak, transforming bail into a substantive punishment (Chen R, 2011, p. 361).

Scholars including Chen Ruihua, Chen Weidong, and Zuo Weimin characterize the PRC's criminal procedure as "investigation-centric," for the very reasons outlined in Chen Ruihua's observations above. Investigation-centrism and the dominance of the case file (which we discuss in more detail in Part 3) operate to support "mutual coordination." It can be argued, of course, that criminal processes in the West, including the UK, are also investigation-centric (McBarnett

1981). Indeed, criminal cases that proceed through the adversarial system of justice in the United States rarely reflect the legal ideal of a contest between equal parties because most cases end up being settled through plea bargaining. Nevertheless, scholars claim that China's policy-implementing mode of criminal procedure—in which police, prosecution, and judicial authorities coordinate their efforts to control crime—places even greater structural limits on the prospects for an equal contest in comparison with other inquisitorial systems (Chen R 2011).

In concluding Part 2, we note from this discussion of scholarly perspectives that how the criminal procedure system in China accommodates both crime control and due process goals is shaped fundamentally by this system's "policy-implementing" purpose. As a vehicle for implementing policy at the hand of the party-state, criminal process sets in place how the judiciary should treat evidence and decide culpability. This process is structured procedurally in the legal system and, through the CPL, is embedded legally in it, to enable this vital task. Let us now turn to how this criminal law process plays out in specific laws, principles, and rights that affect the prospects for a fair criminal trial. In Part 3, we further narrow our focus to the specific debates about fair trial provisions in the law that have remained particularly problematic in the eyes of both Chinese and Western scholars.

3 Three Areas of Concern

In this part, we focus on specific debates over the fair trial process in the CPL. Although the right to a fair trial includes a broad range of rights and procedural guarantees, we selected for closer examination three highly contested areas that continue to generate heated discussion among Chinese legal scholars: the presumption of innocence, interrogational torture, and criminal defense. The three areas of focus highlight some of the key issues discussed earlier: the close nexus among law, justice, and politics, both conceptually and in practice; a fluctuating approach to procedural justice in the context of relatively weak proceduralism in Chinese legal culture; and the importance of, and limits imposed by, China's current institutional setting in the realm of justice. The topics and the three scholarly issues of concern selected here are also important because they represent three of the key and enduring problems in the administration of criminal justice in the PRC that have attracted significant attention inside and outside China, in particular in relation to discussions concerning amendments to the 1979 CPL in 1996 and 2012. These discussions also attest to how Xi Jinping's efforts to advance proceduralism and trial centeredness since

2014 have actually kept in place some of the structural impediments to a fair trial and procedural justice that have characterized Chinese criminal justice at least since the period of reforms began (Chen R 2017; Chen W 2016a; Mou 2017a).

Below we examine how Chinese and Western scholars have conceptualized these three areas since the 1990s, highlighting scholars' attention to changes and continuities in the approach to these knotty problems over the years. We aim to clarify how the approaches to procedural justice and purposes discussed above affect the specifics of pretrial and trial interaction between and among key players in a trial: the defendant, the defense lawyer, the police, the judge, and the prosecutor. We begin this discussion with an analysis of the presumption of innocence, because it provides the conceptual underpinning for the other key issues related to the criminal trial that we discuss here, including the standard of proof, the widespread use of interrogational torture, and the lack of access to legal defense and to justice.[23]

3.1 *The Presumption of Innocence*

Chinese legislation is not rooted in and does not guarantee the presumption of innocence.[24] This omission has been identified as one of the key causes of procedural abuses during pretrial proceedings (Nesossi 2012) and of miscarriages of justice (Jiang 2016). The difficulties in adopting the presumption of innocence relate to the absence of a supportive historical legacy and to the basic ideological and operational principles that underpin the structure of criminal proceedings in the PRC (Jiang 2016; Tian 1999).

The idea of the presumption of innocence had no place in imperial China, where, operating on the basis of a "presumption of guilt" (*youzui tuiding* 有罪推定), defendants were considered guilty until proven innocent (MacCormack 1996). In the mid-1950s, the drafting of a criminal procedural code inspired heated debates among China's legal scholars surrounding the presumption of

23 On the complexity of the concept of the presumption of innocence, see Lippke 2016.

24 The English expression "presumption of innocence" is generally rendered in Chinese as *wuzui tuiding* 无罪推定. However, in the early 1980s, some Chinese scholars reflected upon the use of *tuiding* versus *jiading* 假定 to distinguish between presumption and assumption. In 1983, Lin Xin pointed out that *tuiding* conveys the idea of "inferring" or "deducing." He indicated that the Chinese expression *wuzui tuiding* derived from the Japanese translation of the English expression, but he argued that in Chinese *wuzui tuiding* is inadequate to render properly the English concept of presumption and, as such, is inaccurate. Thus, he suggested the use of *jiading* instead of *tuiding* (Lin 1983). With few exceptions (see Pei 1998), scholarly literature in the 1980s–1990s rarely discussed the distinction again and tended to use the two terms interchangeably (see Fan 1997; Wang 1997; Xiong 1997).

innocence. Their discussions also picked up on the role of defense lawyers, the right to silence, and the right against self-incrimination. These debates stopped during the Anti-Rightist campaigns that began in 1957, when such legal theories were criticized as "bourgeois" (Gelatt 1982). This was the context in which the concept of the presumption of innocence became one of the prime targets of political criticism against "rightists" in the party-state. The approach survived until the end of the Maoist period. This meant that the presumption of innocence was not incorporated into the 1979 CPL, which instead made it the responsibility of the defense to present exculpatory evidence on behalf of the defendant, that is, on presumption of the defendant's guilt (Gelatt 1982).

Thanks to developments in the legal system and in the culture of scholarship, scholars revived the debate over the presumption of innocence during the 1980s and the 1990s. Two main groups emerged. The first comprised scholars who continued to assert that criminal justice should be free of any presumptions. They contended that the principle of the presumption of innocence contradicts the basic tenets of Chinese procedural justice, which asserts the capacity of the criminal justice system to ascertain the truth of a situation and to reach a correct judgment, based on the aphorism "taking the fact as the basis and the law as criterion." Some of these scholars asserted that supporting the principle of a presumption of innocence could even encourage criminal behavior (Wen and Sun 2000; Zhang 1983). The second was made up of scholars who advocated for inclusion of the principle of a presumption of innocence in the CPL, arguing that no contradiction exists between socialist principles on scientific truth and the principle of a presumption of innocence (Chen 1998).

The 1996 revision of the CPL resulted in a compromise between these two divergent views (Huang 1996). The text of the amended CPL did not include any specific reference to the principle of a presumption of innocence but introduced a limited shift in approach toward criminal suspects. Indeed, for the first time the law made the distinction between "criminal suspects" (*fanzui xianyiren* 犯罪嫌疑人) and "defendants" (*beigaoren* 被告人)—the latter being those whom prosecutors had already decided to prosecute. The new nomenclature was meant to indicate a willingness not to prejudge guilt, which by itself does not presume innocence (Hecht 1996, p. 62; Lewis 2012, p. 319). Nevertheless, both the 1979 version of the CPL and the 1996 amended version remained weak in prescribing evidentiary requirements in criminal proceedings (Long 2004). The 1996 revision maintained the original standard of proof that a defendant can be found guilty if "the facts of a case are clear and the evidence reliable and sufficient" (Article 162), but it did not specify the benchmarks for prosecutors to reach in ascertaining a sufficient level of proof. Article 12 of the 1996 CPL states that nobody is to be found guilty without being judged as such by a people's court according to the law. However, as Huang Taiyun (1996) noted, the article should be read as a statement concerning the role of the people's courts in judging guilt, rather than a broader statement about the presumption of innocence.

The introduction of Article 12 and changes in nomenclature led party-state commentators to claim that, through the revision of the 1979 CPL, the PRC had established the principle of a presumption of innocence but also that further work needed to be done to realize this principle in practice (Bing 2011; Lin 2003; Shi 2001; Wen and Sun 2000). The 1996 amendment articles published in the *People's Daily* (*Renmin ribao* 人民日报) in 1997 associated the establishment of the principle of a presumption of innocence with the idea of judicial civilization (*sifa wenming* 司法文明) and stated that the Chinese justice authorities should follow the principle to avoid committing judicial errors and to ensure the protection of suspects' rights (Li F 2003; Pei 2003).

The importance of a presumption of innocence to guarantee the basic procedural rights of criminal suspects and defendants was again discussed in the years leading up to the 2012 amendment to the CPL. Reform proposals drafted by two large cohorts of legal scholars, led respectively by Professor Xu Jingcun at Southwestern University of Political Science and Law (Xinan zhengfa daxue 西南政法大学) and Professor Chen Guangzhong at the China University of Political Science and Law in Beijing (Zhongguo zhengfa daxue 中国政法大学) suggested changes in the wording of Article 12 from "nobody shall be found guilty" to (the defendant) "shall be presumed innocent" (Chen 2004; Xu 2003). They also advocated for the inclusion of a provision stating that "nobody should be compelled to testify against himself or herself or to confess guilt and that no adverse consequences should result from the defendant's refusal to answer questions by the interrogator" (Chen 2002; Hu 2002). A number of scholars also accepted the right to silence (*chenmo quan* 沉默权) and a presumption of innocence but argued that a curtailed form of the right to silence (*xianzhi chenmo quan* 限制沉默权), as discussed in other jurisdictions (e.g., the UK),[25] could be more suitable for China (Nie and Jiang 2002, pp. 226–34). Xu Jingcun (2003, p. 75), for example, suggested that the right to silence and the related principle of a presumption of innocence should be limited and should not be applicable in circumstances in which suspects are charged with national security and public security crimes.

25 Chinese scholars draw the idea of curtailment of the right to silence from the UK 1994 Criminal Justice and Public Order Act. For an overview of the UK 1994 Act and its impact upon the exercise of the right to silence, see Bucke, Street, and Brown 2000; Quirk 2010.

Since the 1996 revision of the CPL, the Chinese scholarly community has continued to advocate that the principle of a presumption of innocence and the related right to silence be established in the CPL to protect the rights of criminal suspects and defendants under the law (Chen et al. 2013; Fan 2016; Wang 2011). Yet the 2012 amended CPL did not incorporate the principle and instead (as discussed below) took initial steps toward clarifying evidentiary burdens in criminal cases.

In 2013 the eighteeenth Central Committee reaffirmed the importance of a presumption of innocence in the administration of criminal justice and encouraged local courts to experiment with new measures to ensure that this presumption is realized in practice. For example, the Henan provincial court experimented with rearranging the configuration of the court during a trial by making criminal suspects sit beside their defense lawyers. It also emphasized that suspects should not cut their hair or wear prison uniforms as if they were offenders (Xu 2013).[26]

The new approach of "placing the trial at the center of criminal proceedings," initiated under Xi Jinping in 2014, has promoted the idea that the criminal trial is the only place in which criminal culpability should be determined. It also endorses two other understandings about trial procedure. The first is that guilt can be determined only by establishing the facts of the case through rigorous testing in court, not merely by presenting in court written testimony in the case file prepared by the police.[27] The second is that the evidence presented in court must be obtained legally.[28] While these are undoubtedly positive developments, they have not substantially altered the situation for criminal suspects and defendants, because, in practice, judges continue to rely heavily, if not exclusively, on written evidence in the police's case file, such as the suspects' confession, transcripts of witness testimony, and material evidence (He J 2013; Zuo 2017).

A defendant's chances of receiving a fair trial can be hindered when witnesses do not appear in court because this prevents the judiciary from having an opportunity to scrutinize evidence other than the contents of the case file, and so it must rely exclusively on written testimony (Mou 2017a). As Wang and Caruso note, the focus on "reading and reviewing documentary evidence does

26 The 2015 SPC Notice on Dress Code of Criminal Defendants and Appellants during the Trial [Guanyu xingshi beigaoren huo shangsuren chuting shoushen shi zhuozhuang wenti de tongzhi 关于刑事被告人或上诉人出庭受审时着装问题的通知] states that criminal suspects should not wear prison uniforms and should not to have their head shaved.

27 The case file is used throughout the entire trial process, from investigation to sentencing.

28 See Joint Opinion 2016.

not allow the trier of fact to adequately judge and assess a witness's credibility, manner and motivations" (2017, p. 64). Yet it is extremely uncommon for witnesses to testify in Chinese courts (McConville et al. 2011; Mou 2017a; Wang and Caruso 2017; Zuo 2017).[29] Even when witnesses appear in court, it is not unusual for them to merely read their written testimony. The judiciary's consequent reliance directly and, in most cases, solely on the written evidence in the case file, both before and during trial, gives this evidence a presumption of legitimacy even though it is not tested or contested through cross examination in court (Chen R 2016, 2017; Chen W 2016a, 2016b; Long 2015).

What is effectively a "presumption of guilt" underlying the authorities' approach to criminal suspects, or at least to the evidence in suspects' cases, often leads judges to exclude evidence collected by the defense that is exculpatory for the defendant (Jiang 2016, p. 245), the aim of which is to avoid "causing contradictory evidence in the file and thus weakening the grounds for a complaint" (Zuo 2017).[30] As a consequence, both the courts and defense lawyers often have no access to exculpatory evidence, leading the defense to concentrate mainly on flaws in the case file (Zuo 2017). A stage-by-stage transfer of the case file from the police to the prosecutor and then from the prosecution to the judge means that "the evidence generated during the previous stage normally constitutes the main body of the case in the next stage" (Zuo 2017, p. 7). Hence, the case file that criminal investigators compile routinely contains all the evidence that judges deem necessary to convict defendants of the crime for which they are indicted. This is partly because of what is called a "unified standard of proof" (*tongyi zhengming biaozhun* 统一证明标准): first the police and then the prosecutor must be satisfied that the standard of proof has been reached before the case proceeds to the next stage of the criminal process, the trial (Chen R 2017; Chen W 2016a).[31]

Until 2012, the standard of proof in the CPL had been that "the facts are clear, and the evidence is reliable and sufficient." However, "reliable and sufficient" couples two subjective and ambiguous terms, neither of which is clarified in the CPL. This "objective" (Long 2004) standard of proof therefore left a great deal of room for elements outside the court—police, prosecutors,

29 According to Article 187 of the 2012 CPL, there is no compunction in law to call a witness if the written testimony is not in dispute.

30 In contrast to provisions in the 1979 CPL, the current 2012 CPL allows the procuratorate to leave exculpatory evidence out of the case file.

31 The standard of proof is the degree of proof identified loosely by the CPL that a judge needs to find a defendant guilty of a crime. For an outline of procedural reforms related to the death penalty, see Biddulph et al. 2017a; for an outline of these reform in relation to the standard of proof in death penalty cases, see Trevaskes 2018.

and party committee members—to shape judicial interpretations about evidence and decisions about culpability in criminal cases (Trevaskes 2012). It was not based on weighing probabilities and was not held up to a benchmark that required judges first to rule out all other possible explanations of the event before guilt could be ascertained (Chen and Liu 2007; Wang J 2015). Because the prosecution's case was routinely put forward as the only explanation of events, "objective truth" was paradoxically truth obtained from highly subjective evidence since exculpable evidence was not routinely included in the case file. Thus, as Cao Zhihua (2008) noted, this position carried the assumption that objective truth would be found, that is, that all the facts that could possibly be gathered about a case could and would be presented in court. But this standard contradicted the reality of how the police and prosecutors represent the truth in the evidence they include in the case file, on the basis of their "presumption of guilt" about the defendant.

In 2012, the CPL was amended to include "beyond a reasonable doubt" as an auxiliary to (and not a substitute for) the original standard of proof that facts are clear and the evidence is reliable (Xiao 2015). However, as Long Zongzhi (2014) claims, this change did not alter the overall nature of the standard of proof, which still relies on the idea of an "objective truth" that can be ascertained through the presentation of written statements sourced from the police investigation, on which judges rely to ascertain the facts of the case. Indeed, without providing judges with directions on how to apply the "reasonable doubt" (*heli huayi* 合理怀疑) principle,[32] the concept remains primarily a theoretical construct that can be used merely "to direct evidentiary thinking" (Long 2014, p. 355) and give the appearance of legitimacy.

According to Chen Ruihua (2014), the SPC authorities maintain that "beyond a reasonable doubt" helps judicial decision-makers focus on the importance of determining the links between various pieces of evidence, to ensure the absence of any major contradiction between them. The SPC's view is that merely by following the general rules of logical deduction and their own decision-making experience, judges should be able to determine that the evidence presented "leaves no room for an alternative explanation of the facts" (Chen R 2014, p. 178). Other leading Chinese jurists argue that the reasonable doubt principle needs to be cultivated in conjunction with improvements in

32 To date, the SPC has not produced a judicial interpretation that defines "beyond a reasonable doubt" or its application.

the evidentiary and procedural norms in general, most notably, the development of a discrete evidence law, which still does not exist in China.[33]

The presumption of innocence principle affects not only conviction-related trial procedures but also the sentencing component of the trial. In recent years, efforts by legal scholars and practitioners to advocate for a separate sentencing procedure have resulted in SPC reforms to procedures that make sentencing relatively independent from conviction-related trial procedures. The scholar Lin Zhiqiu explains the limitations of these changes:

> According to the SPC's newly issued sentencing procedures, after the trial to determine if the defendant is guilty of the charged offence and without rendering a guilty or innocent verdict, the court should immediately proceed to collect the facts and evidence. The relatively separate sentencing process clearly places the defendant in a difficult catch-22 situation. If the defendant chooses to participate in the process of collecting sentencing-related facts and evidence immediately after the trial, this participation could be construed as an admission of guilt and potentially bias the judge's decision. On the other hand, if the defendant chooses not to participate in the process, he/she would forgo the opportunity to participate in sentencing decisionmaking and risk having non-participation interpreted as a reluctance or refusal to cooperate with the court. It is clear that, compared to past practice, the introduction of this relatively separate sentencing process clearly makes no improvement in terms of the defendants' right to participate in the sentencing process.
>
> 2016, p. 362

Therefore, according to Lin (2016, p. 362), sentencing remains in conflict with the idea of a presumption of innocence.

More recently, the presumption of innocence ideal has been challenged in the spate of televised confessions involving what some describe as political prisoners (including civil society activists, journalists, lawyers, publishers, bloggers, and music stars). These shaming events entail coerced public confessions from those who voice views that vary from the party line and are paraded on state television and forced to incriminate themselves by making abject confessions prior to any legal proceedings (Fiskesjö 2017, 2018). Confessions are generally made before trial, often even before formal arrest and forced and extracted through threats and torture (Safeguards

33 For an analysis of the development of evidence law drafts in China, see Li and Wang 2014; Wang and Li 2014; Zhang n.d.; Zhang and Cao 2017; Zhang and Zheng 2014.

Defenders 2018). In violation of both international and domestic law, pressure to confess through public-shaming rituals are but one manifestation of the continuing emphasis in politically sensitive cases to establish guilt outside the courtroom.

3.2 *Interrogational Torture*

In China, interrogational torture has long been regarded as an instrument of crime control, and it was ingrained in the administration of criminal justice for many centuries before the modern era (Nesossi 2012, p. 193). Chinese literature on the history of torture in ancient China is extremely rich and describes specific methods and instruments of judicial torture that were legally approved to secure confessions from criminal suspects.[34] Although officially sanctioned torture was formally abolished in 1905, in Maoist China, especially during the Cultural Revolution, it was widely used to extract confessions from and instill terror among "enemies" (Wang 1997, p. 9).

Notwithstanding the widespread use of torture during criminal proceedings, torture never figured in official or scholarly discussions until around two decades ago (Nesossi 2012, p. 194). According to Chen Yunsheng (2000, pp. 10–11), that torture has remained a sensitive and neglected topic for so long is the result of attempts by the government to maintain its legitimacy intact. Scholars argue that it is also in part the result of a fairly high degree of public tolerance, given the long-standing popular view that suspects are, for all intent and purposes, criminals (Cui 2002).

China has been a signatory of the Convention against Torture and Other Cruel, Inhuman, and Degrading Treatment (CAT) since 1988. However, until the mid-1990s, publications on cases of torture and linked cases of miscarriages of justice were few and far between, limited to internally published reports (Jiang 2016; Nesossi 2017; Trevaskes 2012). In 1992, the Political Department of the MPS (Gong'an bu zhengzhi bu 公安部政治部) published a short collection of cases that involved torture. The volume included eight exemplary cases (*dianxin anli* 典型案例) that underscored the prevalence and seriousness of the problem of torture in the PRC (Political Department of the MPS 1992). That year the MPS also issued the Decision on Resolutely Halting the Practice of Extraction of Confession through Torture by the Police (Guanyu jianjue zhizhi gong'an ganjing xingxun bigong de jueding 关于坚决制止公安干警刑讯逼供的决定), which defined key policies and practical strategies that the public security authorities should implement to put a halt to the practice of torture by the police (Chen R 2014, p. 9). To strengthen the official message against torture and offer the

34 See, e.g., Bao and Ma 1998; Jin 1991; Wang Y 2006; Wang Y 1991.

police practical directions for changing their approach to investigation, at the end of 1995 the MPS also published the Notice on Special Education on Openly Stopping the Practice of Extraction of Confession through Torture (Guanyu jizhong kaizhan zhizhi xingxun bigong zhuanxiang jiaoyu zhengdun de tongzhi 关于集中开展制止刑讯逼供专项教育整顿的通知). This publication exhorted public security bureaus at different levels to establish training courses on the prohibition of torture and to include good anti-torture performance among the evaluation criteria for police officers (Cai 2000; Gao 1998). The extraction of confessions through torture was already prohibited in the 1979 CPL (Article 32) and the Criminal Law of the PRC (Article 136), and a ban on it was included in the revised versions of the laws, respectively, in 1996 (Article 43) and 1997 (Article 247). Yet during this period, scholars continually pointed to the weak enforcement of these articles.

In 1996, the year the CPL was first amended, the MPS organized the first Forum on Specialized Education on Prohibiting the Extraction of Confessions through Torture (Zhizhi xingxun bigong zhuanxiang zhengdun zuotanhui 制止刑讯逼供专项整顿座谈会) to discuss the thirty-one cases of torture that had been uncovered during the year. It also issued the Bulletin on the Public Security Authorities' Specialized Education on Prohibiting the Extraction of Confessions through Torture (Gong'an bu guanyu gong'an jiguan kaizhan zhizhi xingxun bigong zhuanxiang jiaoyu zhengdun de qingkuang tongbao 公安部关于公安机关开展制止刑讯逼供专项教育整顿的情况通报) (Chen 2014, p. 10). That same year, the Supreme People's Procuratorate (SPP) published a report titled *The Crime of Extracting Confessions through Torture* (*Xingxun bigong zui* 刑讯逼供罪), which included analysis of 202 cases of interrogational torture brought to the attention of the SPP by provincial procuratorates and other exemplary cases collected by the SPP's Legal-Disciplinary Office (Faji jianchating 法纪检察厅) (Wang 1997). This report's analysis explained that, although the number of cases of torture peaked during the Cultural Revolution, following the enactment of the 1979 criminal law and the related criminalization of both acts of torture and ill treatment, the use of torture persisted, and an average of 400 cases per year were reported from 1979 to 1989. From 1990 to 1996, the average number of reported cases increased to 420 per year. To indicate the gravity of the problem, the authors also reported that over the period 1993–94, 241 people were tortured to death, and 64 suffered serious physical injuries (Wang 1997, p. 9).

These early accounts of torture, as well as a MPS's 1993 internal publication by Chen Wenqi, discussed in clear terms why torture should be banned as an interrogational practice (Nesossi 2012). They emphasized that torture is deleterious to the image and reputation of the party, the state, and the local government; it can also result in the miscarriage of justice. The report stated that torture should be prohibited because of "the negative influence it has on the masses; the severe harm it causes to the prestige of the party, the government and the public security authorities," and the damage it causes to "the relationship between the party and the masses, and between the police and the people" (Chen 1993, pp. 9–10).

In the early 2000s, PRC scholars and officials began to publicly acknowledge the prevalence of torture (United Nations 2006, p. 14). As Murray Scot Tanner observes, around this time they began "to concede what external observers have long maintained: that torture is a pervasive problem in China's legal-coercive apparatus" (2000, p. 13). Since then, the literature on the issue has become increasingly detailed, and the problem of torture has been discussed in various domestic legal publications (Nesossi 2012, 2017; Sapio 2010). Senior officials and scholars started to admit that torture and ill treatment of detainees, especially with the aim of extracting confessions, was a common and persistent problem in the justice system and that it could not be ignored or condoned as a necessary evil of the criminal justice system (Cui 2002, p. 333; Li H 2003, p. 146; Zhou 1999). Scholarly debate was accompanied by an increasingly large and sophisticated corpus of legislative documents at different levels of authority, covering three main issues: the prohibition of torture, punishment of perpetrators, and exclusion of evidence extracted through torture. Indeed, since the 1990s, scholars and legal reformers alike began to consider combating torture through legislation as vital to making the country progress to a system governed by law, moving away from a regime perennially at the mercy of police authorities bent on "striking hard" at crime (Belkin 2011; Lewis 2011; Nesossi 2017; Tanner 2000; Trevaskes 2012).

The central issue in debates on torture in China over the past two decades has been "interrogational torture for extracting confessions from criminal suspects." The expression "extraction of confessions through torture" (*xingxun bigong* 刑讯逼供) is the preferred terminology, rather than the more straightforward term "torture" (*kuxing* 酷刑) (Jin 2007, pp. 2–3; Wang G 2007, p. 276).[35] Arguably this may indicate authorities' unwillingness to face up to the prevalence of the "torture" problem not just for extracting confessions but across the board within the justice system. In fact, as Chinese scholars have noted, the expression *xingxun bigong* restricts the scope of torture to the practice of coerced confession exclusively in criminal proceedings. Although this is the

35 The official Chinese term for Convention against Torture (CAT) is simply *kuxing*, rather than *xingxun bigong* or any longer expression that explicitly references the Convention against Torture.

most prevalent manifestation of torture in contemporary China (Chen 2000, p. 12; Min 2002, p. 291), it certainly does not encompass all the forms of torture and other cruel, inhuman, or degrading treatments or punishments that are reported in administrative cases or cases handled by the party's disciplinary departments. It may also not encapsulate other instances of torture conducted within the criminal justice system that have escaped official censure or even detection. This is also contrary to the definition of torture in Article 1 of the CAT, which includes three essential elements: the act of torture amounts to the infliction of severe mental or physical pain or suffering; it is perpetrated by or with the consent or acquiescence of state authorities; and it is committed with a specific purpose, such as gaining information, punishment, or intimidation.

Limiting the term "torture" to refer to tortuous acts conducted only for a specific purpose and primarily in pretrial procedures has consequences. It enables other instances of torture—for other purposes or reasons and at other stages of the criminal procedure—to be ignored or downplayed. As leading criminal justice scholar Zhao Bingzhi (2003, pp. 161–64) notes, the expression *xingxun bigong* can be used only in criminal cases. By definition, therefore, it excludes cases of torture in administrative punishment proceedings. Regardless of the tortuous treatment meted out in administrative cases—the torturing of sex workers, for example—this treatment is not considered a form of *xingxun bigong*. In these cases, it is acknowledged as a crime of "extracting testimony by force" (*baoli quzheng* 暴力取证).[36] Indeed, before its 2012 amendment, the CPL itself did not provide a comprehensive definition of torture in line with international standards. It did not contain references to forms of psychological torture and, contrary to international requirements, did not criminalize both attempts to commit torture and acts of complicity or participation in torture (Chen R 2008).[37]

After the turn of the twenty-first century, Chinese scholarly debate has gradually shifted its focus from identifying the causes of or reasons for torture to trying to combat it. The new focus concerns how to treat evidence obtained through torture. This shift followed attempts by legislators to enhance sanctions for torture in various drafts of amendments to the CPL during the 2000s.

The two central issues troubling legal scholars in the 2000s were apparent weakness in the enforcement of existing laws against torture and the

36 Article 247 of the 1997 Criminal Law.

37 For a comprehensive overview of Chinese debates on the definition of torture in contemporary China, see Jin 2007.

unwillingness of party officials to act on their own condemnation of the widespread use of torture within criminal procedure. Scholars such as Zuo Weimin and Zhou Hongbo (2002) attempted to explain the reluctance of state officials to make solid and lasting improvements to the situation in a way that is consistent with changing social (including scholarly) attitudes on the use of torture by legal authorities. In particular, they explained the situation in relation to China's stage of modernization in the early twenty-first century. They contended that the state was transitioning from a "power-assertive" state (*xuanyao quanlixin guojia* 炫耀权力型国家) to a modern "routine supervision—based" system (*richang jianduxin guojia* 日常监督型国家). In practice, this meant that while the state remained "power assertive," the Chinese public was increasingly demanding party-state accountability through supervision. Thus, on the one hand, the debate on torture was becoming progressively more open and torture more widely condemned. On the other, however, to maintain its power and to control society, the party-state continued to rely on coercive measures. Through the reluctance of politicolegal authorities to punish torturers, the party-state was tacitly encouraging police officers to continue to strike hard against crime and to solve cases hastily as per the prevailing Strike Hard criminal justice policy (Zuo and Zhou 2002, pp. 37–40).

This situation continued throughout the 2000s. Party leaders continued to condemn torture and continued to set up initiatives to improve the situation, however, they were reluctant to give the CPL meaningful enforcement teeth to sanction those who committed torture. To show their willingness to counteract abusive police practices that were contrary to the spirit of the Hu-era "harmonious justice" agenda, central government authorities supported local experiments aimed at limiting opportunities for the police to use torture to extract confession from criminal suspects and defendants. In 2006, one particularly well-known experiment led to the introduction of audiovisual recording in a number of police stations around the country.[38] Eminent scholars such

38 The first experiment of audiovisual registration took place in Zhejiang province in 1997 and was administered by the Zhejiang procuratorial authorities in relation to duty crimes. In 2005–2006, the SPP declared its plan to extend the Zhejiang experiment to the whole country and issued three key documents that formalized the use of audio-video recording of interrogations of criminal suspects involved in duty crimes: the SPP Regulations on the Implementation of Audiovisual Recording Technologies during Interrogation of Criminal Suspects in Duty Crimes (For Trial Implementation) [*Jiancha jiguan xunwen zhiwu fanzui xianyiren shixing quan luyin luxiang jishu guifan* (*shixing*) 检察机关讯问职务犯罪嫌疑人实行全录音录像技术规范（试行）] (December 2005); the SPP Developments on the Implementation of Audiovisual Registration Technologies during Interrogation of Criminal Suspects (For Trial Implementation) [*Xunwen quancheng tongbu luyin luxiang xitong jishu gongzuo liucheng* (*shixing*) 询问全程同步录音录

as Chen Weidong (Chen and Xu 2008) and Fan Chongyi (2005, 2007) became involved in various pilot projects in the mid-2000s, coordinated by foreign donors to explore the application of these measures in the Chinese context. Chen and Xu (2008, pp. 106–8) in particular claimed that digital recording could be an effective supervisory instrument to limit interrogational torture and to provide support for frontline police officers involved in interrogation who could use audiovisual recording to prove that they are law abiding. Although national media claimed this was a fundamental breakthrough in preventing torture in China (She 2007a, 2007b; Wang X 2007a, 2007b; Wu and Liu 2007), others noted that this technical innovation was implemented in a patchy way, only in major cases, and even then not for the entire interview but only to record the final confession (Chen and Spronken 2012; McConville et al. 2011; Nesossi 2017).

One key factor leading to the Chinese authorities' progressively more resolute rejection of torture in the 2000s was the disclosure of several cases of miscarriages of justice caused by the use of torture and ill treatment to coerce confessions from criminal suspects and defendants (Belkin 2011, 2017; Chen and Spronken 2012; He 2016; He and He 2012; Huang 2012; Jiang 2016; Lewis 2011; Nesossi 2016, 2017). For example, Du Peiwu, a former police officer, was wrongly convicted of the murder of his wife and a police officer, and the sentence was based on his false confession extracted through torture. During his trial, he claimed to have been beaten, hanged with handcuffed wrists, and shocked with a cattle prod. In November 2000, Du was released after a group of car thieves confessed to the murders. One year after the disclosure of the case of Du's wrongful conviction, the SPP issued the Notice on Strictly Prohibiting the Use of Confession Extracted through Torture as the Basis for Conviction (Guanyu yanjin jiang xingxun bigong huoqu de fanzui xianyiren gongshu zuowei ding'an yiju de tongzhi 关于严禁将刑讯逼供获取的犯罪嫌疑人供述作为定案依据的通知) which, for the first time, required the procuratorate to "resolutely exclude" confessions obtained through coercive or other unlawful means. The Notice precipitated discussion among leading criminal justice scholars, such as Chen Weidong, Song Yinghui, and Cui Min, to argue for more detailed exclusionary rules, to learn from anti-torture measures in

像系统技术工作流程 （试行）] (December 2006), and the SPP Regulations on the Establishment of Technologies for Implementing the System of Audiovisual Recording during Interrogation [*Xunwen quancheng tongbu luyin luxiang xitong jianshe jishu guifan (shixing)* 询问全程同步录音录像系统建设技术规范 （试行）] (December 2006). The MPS, following the example of the SPP, in 2005 carried out the first experiment on audio-video recording in police stations in Yunnan Province. See Fan 2007.

practice internationally, and to take into account both theoretical and practical perspectives on the matter (see Chen 2006; Chen and Xu 2008; Cui 2009; Song 2007).

In the early 2000s, many scholars predicted the imminent arrival of a long-awaited exclusionary rule for coerced confession (Belkin 2011, p. 285), but this did not come until 2010. Legislation addressing the issue of the exclusion of evidence coerced through torture was enacted nearly ten years after the Du case, in the aftermath of another notorious miscarriage of justice that had sparked a national uproar: the Zhao Zuohai case (Nesossi 2016). After serving eleven of the twenty-nine years of imprisonment to which he had been sentenced, Zhao was exonerated after his alleged murder victim, Zhao Zhanshang, "returned from the dead" to their home village to claim social welfare benefits (Chen H 2010; Chen R 2010; Pei 2010). In 2010, just a month after media reports on Zhao's case, China's justice authorities, including the SPC, the SPP, the MPS, the Ministry of State Security, and the Ministry of Justice, enacted the Two Regulations (Liangge guiding 两个规定) addressing the issue of exclusion: the Regulations on Several Issues Concerning Examining and Evaluating Evidence in Capital Cases (Guanyu banli sixing anjian shencha panduan zhengju ruogan wenti de guiding 关于办理死刑案件审查判断证据若干问题的规定) and the Regulations on Several Issues Concerning the Exclusion of Illegally Obtained Evidence in Criminal Cases (Guanyu banli xingshi anjian yange paichu feifa zhengju ruogan wenti de guiding 关于办理刑事案件严格排除非法证据若干问题的规定).

Margaret Lewis's work on the Two Regulations is the most detailed and nuanced study on this important breakthrough in anti-torture legislation. Lewis (2011) explains that the Rules were the outcome of increasing public dissatisfaction with the criminal justice system, resulting from miscarriages of justice and police abuse in places of detention, as well as international factors. Indeed, she argues that "a commitment by the leadership in Beijing to an exclusionary rule has positive public relations potential overseas as a response to reports of government abuses" and complements "discussions regarding China's long-awaited ratification of the International Covenant on Civil and Political Rights (ICCPR)" (Lewis 2011, p. 629). Broadly speaking, as Lewis claims, "both at home and abroad, the PRC Government stands to gain political capital by taking a clear stance against police abuse and the use of illegally obtained evidence to secure convictions" (2011, p. 679).

The 2010 Regulations set out three key changes. First, lawyers and their clients were given the right to request a pretrial hearing to consider allegations that a confession had been illegally obtained, at which they had to provide supporting evidence to show that torture had taken place. Second, the regulations gave the procuratorate responsibility for proving that evidence had been obtained lawfully. Third, investigators who had allegedly committed torture may now be called to testify as witnesses in court (Nesossi 2012).

Chinese scholars enthusiastically applauded the issuing of the Two Regulations in 2010 but pointed out the difficulties concerning the application of these regulations in judicial practice (Chen 2010; Li 2012; Long 2010; Song and Wang 2010). Three particularly contentious issues emerged. The first was the scope of exclusion in relation to material evidence—that is, whether material evidence obtained illegally should be excluded fully or could be retained in part. Because the legislation is still heavily focused on the exclusion of oral evidence, uncertainty remains about the weight of physical and documentary evidence and its relationship to the confession (Chen and Guo 2014). The second concerned the indirect issue of the burden of proof—that is, whether the burden should be exclusively on the procuratorate or shared between the procuratorate and the defendant. This was seen as particularly problematic in view of lawyers' weak role during pretrial proceedings (as explained in the section below) and their inability to collect evidence to substantiate their clients' torture claims. The third related to the weak definition of torture in the Regulations, which, scholars argued, do not list all the circumstances according to international standards and leave significant discretionary power of interpretation to judicial authorities.

In addition to the the difficulties specifically related to judicial proceedings, the 2010 Regulations were not considered relevant to cases that were administered through the party's disciplinary processes in extralegal measures, such as *shuanggui* 双规.[39] As Human Rights Watch reported in 2016, this practice gives the Central Commission on Discipline Inspection (CCDI)[40] the authority to summon Party's members at a "designated location at a designated time" (Human Rights Watch 2016). The Report suggests that suspects are deprived of their liberty for an unspecified length of time, interrogated, and, in some cases, repeatedly tortured. After a confession is obtained, some suspects are then transferred to the regular criminal justice system for prosecution (Human Rights Watch 2016).

Beyond these difficulties were the continuing problems concerning defendants' access to defense lawyers (see below) and weaknesses in the system of audiovisual recording. Jeremy Daum (2011, p. 711) claimed the Rules "represent a series of half-measures, likely the result of compromise among the drafting agencies; they make grand gestures toward procedural fairness, only

39 *Shuanggui* is an investigative measure used by Party discipline organs on members of the CCP suspected of criminal offences, corruption or misconduct. See Sapio 2008.

40 On recent changes to the CCDI, see Li 2017.

to stop short of demanding it." Yet, two years after their promulgation, the Two Regulations were embedded in the 2012 amendment of the CPL. Not surprisingly, the three issues mentioned above in relation to the Two Regulations continued to be debated after the CPL's amendment (see Biddulph et al. 2017a; Gong 2016; Guo 2017; He J 2013; Wu 2014).

Xi Jinping was China's first leader to make the prevention of miscarriages of justice central *yifa zhiguo* governance platform following the disclosure of numerous miscarriages of justice in 2012 and 2013. At the beginning of his administration, the issue of excluding illegally obtained evidence once again began to feature prominently in both scholarly and official writings. Under Xi, the Decisions of the third and fourth CCP plenums in 2013 and 2014 also highlighted the strict prohibition on torture. The importance of strengthening audiovisual recording was also highlighted in the 2014 Resolution of the fourth plenum of the eighteenth party congress under the general theme of the rule of law. On June 14, 2016, the MPS issued the Regulations Concerning the Public Security Authorities using Audio-Video Methods to Record Their Work (Gong'an jiguan xianchang zhifa shiyin pin jilu gongzuo guiding 公安机关现场执法视音频记录工作规定). The Regulations list specific circumstances in which the audiovisual recording should be used, including all the investigative procedures in administrative and criminal cases. They highlight that recordings should be made from the very beginning to the very end of the procedures. If, for any external reason (faulty recorder, weather conditions, or other reasons), the recording is interrupted and not resumed, explanations should be given in a relevant written report. It states that the recording should be properly stored for a minimum of six months, and, if it constitutes evidence in administrative and criminal cases, it should be stored forever.

In 2013 and 2014, government and legal authorities issued a series of legal and political documents that specifically addressed the causes of judicial errors, identified avenues for ascertaining individual responsibilities, and examined systemic problems in the justice system. The 2013 Political-Legal Committee Provisions on Preventing Miscarriage of Justice (Guanyu qieshi fangzhi yuanjia cuo'an de guiding 关于切实防止冤假错案的规定) stress that instances of torture and extraction of confessions through violent means should be punished severely according to the law. Attention given to the issue in 2013 placed a spotlight squarely on procedural requirements for courts in handling cases with weak evidence. It provides for the exclusion of evidence obtained through torture or other illegal means (paragraph 3), the strict examination and cross-examination of evidence in court as the basis for conviction (paragraph 6), and implementation of the legal standard of proof (paragraph 7).

Similar points were made in the SPC Opinions on Preventing Miscarriages of Justice (Guanyu jianli jianquan fangfan xingshi yuanjia cuo'an gongzuo jizhi de yijian 关于建立健全防范刑事冤假错案工作机制的意见, issued November 21, 2013). These Opinions require judges to follow legal procedures strictly. They reminded appeals courts that they are responsible for counterchecking judgments in cases where the evidence is sketchy or the facts are unclear. Importantly, the document identifies two criteria not included in the 2010 and 2012 legislation to define illegally obtained evidence: first, when the confession by the defendant is obtained outside a legal place of detention; and second, when the full confession has not been recorded using an audiovisual recording system. Confessions so obtained are considered "nonvoluntary" and, as a result, should be excluded.

In addition to the measures outlined above, the party-state has also issued changes in the judicial, procuratorial, and police responsibility systems in relation to misjudged cases, to extend responsibility across a decision-maker's lifetime. Since the fourth plenum in 2014, the SPC, the SPP, and the Ministry of Justice have all announced regulations on lifetime responsibility, to enhance their accountability systems. But, as the scholar Jiang Su notes, these changes have not created new accountability systems that operate beyond the existing (institutional) self-examination and self-investigation procedures. Hence, senior authorities have relatively limited motivation to investigate and affix responsibility for wrongful decisions. As Jiang explains, although accountability procedures have improved, the organs responsible for initiating the procedure for investigation of the judiciary are still internal bodies, rather than external independent or impartial agencies (Jiang 2018).

Perhaps the best-publicized move to enhance judicial accountability and the fair trial in the Xi era to date is the promotion of "placing the trial at the center of criminal proceedings." As outlined in Part 1 of this paper, to highlight the existing corpus of legislation, in October 2016, five central authorities—the SPC, the SPP, the MPS, the MSS, and the Ministry of Justice—issued a joint opinion that reinforced the principle of placing the trial at the center of criminal proceedings. The 2016 Opinion on Trial Centeredness and the SPC's 2017 Implementing Opinions on Comprehensively Promoting the Criminal Proceedings Reforms of Placing the Trial at the Center (Guanyu quanmian tuijin yishenpan wei zhongxin de xingshi susong zhidu gaige de shishi yijian 关于全面推进以审判为中心的刑事诉讼制度改革的实施意见) obligate the procuratorate in certain important cases to directly question criminal suspects about whether their confession had been coerced or if they were aware that any evidence for their cases had been collected illegally.[41] In June 2017, the same bodies issued Regulations on Several Issues Concerning the Strict Exclusion of Illegal Evidence in Handling Criminal Cases (Guanyu

41 For a critique of the February 2017 Regulations, see Daum 2017.

banli xingshi anjian yange paichu feifa zhengju ruogan wenti de guiding 关于办理刑事案件严格排除非法证据若干问题的规定), which once again reiterate provisions excluding evidence obtained by torture. Jeremy Daum (2017) argues that these provisions will not substantially protect against the possibility of interrogational torture because the exclusionary rules still do not contain a "fruit of the poisonous tree" doctrine, excluding all evidence derived from an initial violation.

Notwithstanding the renewed emphasis on combating torture and excluding coerced evidence, scholars have continued to express skepticism about the extent of change that new legal provisions introduce in judicial and police practice. Chen Weidong (2017), for example, notes that the new "trial-centered" approach will not make a significant impact on addressing the issue of torture during trial proceedings. The 2016 Opinion on Trial Centeredness indeed requires that all interrogations be audiovisually recorded (Joint Opinion 2016). But in Chen's view, this practice will not make a significant difference because the process of recording is controlled by the police or the procuratorate, who may selectively record only those parts of the interrogations where the criminal suspects confess to the crime, rather than the full interrogation. Their aim is to support their investigative practices, rather than to protect the rights of criminal suspects or offenders. Daum (2017) also notes that the aim of excluding evidence is primarily to avoid miscarriages of justice, rather than to deter police misconduct.

In fact, the 2016 and 2017 Opinions and Regulations do not obviate some of the problems already visible in the 2010 Two Regulations or the 2012 CPL. They do not contain a "fruit of the poisonous tree doctrine," which would allow judges to exclude all evidence obtained from an initial violation. They do not give defendants better access to lawyers during pretrial proceedings, and lawyers are still prohibited from attending interrogations and checking audiovisual recordings. And they do not compel a court appearance by investigators whom the court summons when it identifies the need to resolve doubts about the legality of the investigative tactics. But, as Daum (2017) explains, "this rarely happens."

Analysis by Hu Zhifeng (2017, pp. 38–40) refers to a 2013 survey that demonstrates that a significant number of errors, such as damaging or illegal editing of audiovisual files, are very common. Hu explains that most police officers who damage recorded files face very light or no punishment, which makes scholars question the effectiveness of such measures. This happens not only because the police are not particularly concerned about the issue but also because existing laws and regulations do not stipulate precise penalties for this kind of conduct. Neither the 2016 Opinion nor the 2017 Provisions provide new rules regarding the criminal punishment of torture.

Other scholars have focused on the difficulty of making exclusionary rules effective in practice. Biddulph et al. (2017a, pp. 106–8) highlight four main areas that remain at the center of scholarly contention today. The first concerns legislation prohibiting torture and regulating the exclusion of illegally obtained evidence. The legislation contains numerous ambiguities in relation to the scope and definition of torture (Guo 2015, 2017) and leaves considerable discretion to individual judges (Chen and Guo 2014; Guo 2015, 2017; Yang and Chen 2015). Second, a lack of clarity remains concerning the procedures adopted to exclude evidence, the very high standards set to prove that torture has been committed, and the lack of remedial actions that can be pursued when a judge considers an application for exclusion of evidence (Wang 2015). The third is the continuing weak role of the defense (discussed below) (Liang and He 2014; Liang et al. 2016). The fourth is the continuing close institutional dynamics among the police, the procuratorate, and the courts, which effectively give the police protective cover. The significant power of the police continues to make the process of seeking responsibility for alleged torture particularly problematic (Liu and Halliday 2011, 2016; Nesossi 2017).

Western scholars, including Margaret Lewis (2011), Joshua Rosenzweig (2011, 2013, 2017), Jeremy Daum (2017), Fu Hualing and Richard Cullen (2008, 2011), Elisa Nesossi (2017), Flora Sapio (2010), and Eva Pils (2014, 2017), have followed recent developments in Chinese legislation and the relevant debates by Chinese scholars in the late Hu era and current Xi period. Under Xi, and following the disappearances and trials of eminent human rights lawyers and activists, the issue of torture has been routinely covered in Western media outlets. Scholars note that, notwithstanding increasingly sophisticated legislation, torture is still widespread in both common criminal cases and cases involving human rights activists (Nesossi and Franceschini 2018; Pils 2017). Rights-protection (*weiquan* 维权) lawyers detained or harassed in the human rights crackdown beginning in July 2015 have revealed the ordeals and violence to which they were subject while in detention (Gan 2017). Western observers have noted that, despite the robust corpus of legislation prohibiting torture, Chinese authorities wielded numerous types of torture or inhuman and degrading treatment against the lawyers and defendants held in the 2015 crackdown (China Human Rights Lawyers Concern Group 2017).

3.3 *Criminal Defense Lawyers*

China's approach to the role of lawyers in criminal trials has been significantly influenced by historical attitudes toward the practice of defense and social indifference to, and intolerance of, criminal suspects. Lawyers were an alien concept in ancient China, and when the profession emerged at the end of the sixteenth century, they were derogatorily labeled "litigation tricksters" (*songgun* 讼棍) (Dang 2005; Fuma 2007; Macauley 1998). In spite of the persistence of this negative attitude, authorities in Republican China attempted to improve the conditions of the legal profession (Conner 1994). But after 1949, and in circumstances similar to those of their colleagues in other communist countries, lawyers were harshly criticized and purged for representing the interests of their clients—the "enemies" (Alford 1996, p. 27; Li 1977). Since the beginning of the 1980s, lawyers have progressively gained more strength, independence, and professional autonomy.[42] This has coincided with the creation of the Chinese bar in 1986 (the All-China Lawyers Association [Quanguo lüshi xiehui 全国律师协会]) and the enactment of the Lawyers Law ten years later (Alford 2001; Li 2000; Liu S 2007; Zhu 2004).

The late 1990s was an important period for the development of legislation relating to criminal defense lawyers. Before the introduction of the Lawyers Law in 1996, the party-state classified lawyers as "state legal workers" (*guojia falü gongzuozhe* 国家法律工作者). As such, they were subordinate to the state and its institutions, and their aim was to provide "legal assistance to government, enterprises, social associations, and citizens" as well as to safeguard "the interests of the state and collectives and the lawful rights and interests of citizens" (Article 1 of the 1980 Provisional Regulations of the PRC on Lawyers).[43] After 1996, at least on paper, lawyers were no longer referred to as "state legal workers," and most became private practitioners. Enactment of the CPL that year introduced provisions to support lawyers' professionalization while still keeping their autonomy under scrutiny (Fu 1998; Sheng 2003; Yu 2002; Zhu 2004). The legislation attempted to open up some room for independent action for lawyers, empowering them to act both as legal counsel (*falü zixun* 法律咨询) and in a defense role (*daili bianhu* 代理辩护). At the same time, however, the existing institutional power structure remained, in which lawyers

42 The 1982 Chinese Constitution spells out "the right to defense" in Article 125.

43 Under the 1979 CPL, lawyers had no right to provide legal services to a suspect under investigation, and were specifically barred from meeting suspects in custody until both the police and the prosecutors had finished their investigation and transferred it to the court.

continued to be perceived as outsiders to the police—prosecutor—court (*gongjianfa* 公检法) trifecta (Liang et al. 2014; Liu 2011; Sheng 2003).[44]

Scholars including Sida Liu and Terence Halliday (2016), Jonathan Benney (2013), Eva Pils (2014), Ethan Michelson (2006), and Fu Hualing and Richard Cullen (2008, 2011) have written extensively on the political bulwarks to providing effective defense counsel. After the mid-1990s, debates among Chinese legal scholars and lawyers focused primarily on the "three difficulties" (*san da nan* 三大难) and the issue of the "big stick 306" (306 *da bang* 306 大棒) (Michelson 2006). The first refers to the difficulties that criminal defense lawyers encounter in organizing meetings with criminal suspects and defendants in detention (*huijian dangshiren/beigaoren nan* 会见当事人/被告人难), gaining access to the files of the procuratorate (*yuejuan fuyin nan* 阅卷复印难), and collecting evidence (*quzheng nan* 取证难) and cross-examining witnesses at trial (*zhizheng nan* 质证难). Some scholars and legal practitioners have also talked about "ten difficulties," adding to the previous ones the difficulty of obtaining bail, getting witnesses to appear in court, getting a hearing for appellate trial, pleading innocence, participating in the process of death penalty review, abolishing Article 306 of the Criminal Law, and proving that evidence was illegally obtained (Sun 2011). The expression "big stick 306" refers to the use of Article 306 of the 1997 Criminal Law prohibiting the falsification of evidence by lawyers and the crime of perjury (Halliday and Liu 2007; Liu and Halliday 2016).

With each revision of both the CPL and the Lawyers Law,[45] Chinese scholars have looked closely at how the amended legislation may improve the work of lawyers in these areas.[46] Most Chinese scholars link their analyses to the wider discourse on the protection of criminal suspects' individual rights and respect for international standards (Fan and Gu 2007; Gu 2012; Liu et al. 2007). In contrast, official publications and statements by the public security authorities consider how criminal defense rights could negatively affect social stability. They contend that lawyer—client meetings at the pretrial stage, for example,

---

44 Article 96 of the 1996 CPL provided that after the first interrogation or from the day on which compulsory measures are adopted, criminal suspects are allowed to appoint a lawyer to provide them with legal advice and to file petitions and complaints on their behalf. Article 32 stated that criminal suspects or defendants may exercise their right to defend themselves or appoint a defender who may or may not be a lawyer. Moreover, according to Article 33, suspects have the right to be defended and to appoint a defense lawyer from the date on which their case is transferred to the procuratorate for examination.

45 The 1996 Lawyers Law was revised in 2007.

46 Considering amendments to the CPL and the role of lawyers, Liu and Halliday (2009) elaborate on the concept of recursivity of law to explain why the law has cycled through numerous reforms without improving the conditions of lawyers' criminal defense work.

have the potential to hamper investigators' ability to conduct investigations effectively and to obtain a truthful confession from criminal suspects (Bai and Cheng 2008; Guan 2008).

Scholars note that lawyers face the "three difficulties" for several reasons. Two of the most obvious reasons are the resistance by detention authorities, the police, and the procuratorate; and inconsistencies and loopholes in the legislation, for example, between the 1990 Criminal Detention Regulations, the 1996 and 2012 CPL, and the 2007 Lawyers Law. Publications by the numerous scholars working in this area include Liu (1997), Yang (2008), Jiao and Chen (2008), Liu (2008), Wang (2008), Wang and Meng (2008), Chen Ruihua (2008), and Fang and Zhang (2005). Scholars such as Guan (2008) report that to organize meetings with their clients, lawyers often need the approval of both the authorities handling the case—that is, the public security authorities, the procuratorate, and the courts—and the authorities administering detention centers, under the unjustified pretext that theirs is a "case involving state secrets" (*guojia mimi anjian* 国家秘密案件).[47]

One of the most debated issues after the 2007 amendment of the Lawyers Law concerned the monitoring of meetings between criminal suspects and their lawyers. Indeed, the 2007 Lawyers Law requires that meetings between lawyers and their clients "should not be monitored" (*bu bei jianting* 不被监听). However, the expression "should not be monitored" is left unqualified, hence open to various differing interpretations (Cheng 2008, p. 3). While the police interpret it as "not using instruments of surveillance" (*bu tongguo shebei jianting* 不通过设备监听), thus allowing the police or the procuratorate to be on site during the meeting without infringing the legislation, scholars interpret the provision as implying that the police and the procuratorate cannot be on site and cannot observe the meeting without listening to the meeting content (Meng 2011; Wang and Meng 2008, p. 6).

Scholarly reflections five years after the 2012 amendment of the CPL and in the context of Xi's trial-centered agenda indicate that the role of lawyers in the criminal justice system remains precarious. Chen (2017) notes that official interpretation of the idea of "placing the trial at the center of criminal proceedings" basically ignores the key role of the lawyer in fostering greater opportunities for judicial fairness. At least in theory, provisions in the 2012 CPL allow suspects to retain a defense lawyer at the investigative stage of the criminal process.

47 While in average cases lawyers do not need authorities' approval to meet their clients in detention, investigative authorities are required to approve both the appointment of a lawyer by a criminal suspect and all subsequent meetings between the lawyer and the client. The responsibility for approval is thus still with the authorities.

These provisions also allow lawyers to meet their clients without the approval of the police in most cases (with the exception of cases that authorities identify as involving national security, terrorism, or particularly serious bribery). The Law also protects against police monitoring of lawyer-client at detention centers, and, most notably, in theory, gives lawyers greater access to the prosecution's case file.

However, as Biddulph et al. (2017a) note, the CPL still fails to give defense lawyers the right to undertake independent investigation of a case. As Guo Zhiyuan points out, it remains difficult for the defense to collect evidence to contest the prosecution's claims via independent investigation (Guo 2014). Neither the 2016 Joint Opinion on Trial Centeredness nor the 2017 SPC Implementing Opinion on Trial Centeredness contains any provisions that substantially improve a suspect's access to a lawyer at one of the most crucial stages of the process: the interrogation. Weaknesses in the legislation are reflected in practice, as relevant empirical research indicates. At the pretrial stage, lawyers still have significant difficulty in meeting their clients, accessing case files, and gathering evidence (Han 2015; Liu and Halliday 2016). During the criminal trial, their role is often considered a mere formality, leading some authors to define it as purely a performance without substantive value (Li L 2015).

The threat of the "big stick 306" mentioned above has also attracted significant interest and concern among Chinese and Western scholars since the early 2000s, in particular, before the more recent abrupt repression of the legal community under Xi Jinping. Article 306 is similar to Article 38 in the 1996 CPL (now Article 42 in the 2012 CPL)[48] and Article 40(6) in the 2007 Lawyers Law, which prohibits perjury and the falsification of evidence by lawyers.[49] Chinese and Western scholars note that these provisions seriously jeopardize the ability to mount a meaningful criminal defense because they make challenging the evidence provided by the prosecution risky business for a lawyer (UN Commission on Human Rights, Civil, and Political Rights 2006). According to

48 Article 38 was amended in the 2012 CPL to highlight that not only lawyers could falsify evidence. The revised article states that it is illegal "for defense lawyers *or any other person* to falsify or suppress evidence or induce others to do so" (emphasis added).

49 Specifically, the articles prohibit lawyers from destroying or falsifying evidence and from "coercing or luring witnesses" into changing their testimony. Article 306 generally applies to situations in which witnesses recant confessions they made at an earlier stage, and it is often invoked to intimidate and sanction lawyers on a charge of perjury when the defendant or the witnesses have misrepresented facts to them, fabricated evidence without the lawyers' knowledge, or claimed that earlier statements to investigators were made under duress or were inaccurate (Nesossi 2012, p. 153).

Liu and Halliday, the logic of this article is straightforward: "a witness gives testimony to the police. When questioned by the defendant's lawyer, the witness changes his testimony. Police allege that the change in testimony shows that the lawyer induced the witnesses to lie or present false testimony, and as a result it follows that the lawyer is obstructing justice" (2016, p. 59).

Fu Hualing (2007) explains two factors that resulted in the insertion of Article 306 in the 1997 Criminal Law and of Article 38 in the 1996 CPL, which were a compromise between different institutional actors in the criminal justice system and the significant change in status of lawyers and law firms since the mid-1990s. Indeed, both legislative provisions were intended as instruments to keep defense lawyers in check. Fu (2007) argues that "falsifying evidence" became the weapon of choice to prosecute lawyers as soon as it was introduced, replacing the use of embezzlement charges, but the number of prosecutions against lawyers has not increased overall. Fu points out that retaliatory prosecutions also reflect that lawyers "have become more proactive, aggressive and innovative in defending the rights of their clients and of themselves, posing serious legal challenges that the prosecution has never encountered before" (2007, p. 96).

Since the late 1990s, concerns over cases involving criminal lawyers have generated "a vigorous and emotional debate" over Article 306, which has long been considered the sword of Damocles hanging over a lawyer's head (Cheng 2006, p. 335; Michelson 2003). Liu and Halliday (2016, p. 58) explain that the prospective crime of perjury by lawyers is an intimidating "big stick" held over lawyers' evidence collection because of the dual identity of the procuratorate acting as both prosecutor and supervisor in the criminal trial. During the 2000s, several Chinese scholars and media commentators reported cases in which criminal defense lawyers were detained and prosecuted on the basis of Articles 306 and 307 in the Criminal Law (Chen and Mo 2008; Du 2002; Li Hongbing 2003; Liu 2003; Wu 2004).[50] Although some have argued that Article 306 should not be repealed because the problem lies in its misuse rather than its substance, others contend that when lawyers, judges, and the procuratorate cooperate to achieve justice, Article 306 will become an innocuous legal provision (Deng and Wang 2003). Still other scholars argue that harassment of criminal defense lawyers will not cease simply by repealing Article 306

50 An unpublished survey by the All-China Lawyers Association revealed that, between 1997 and 2002 over 500 lawyers were detained, accused, or sanctioned for falsification of evidence, but that 80 percent of them were later cleared of any wrongdoing (Human Rights Watch 2008, p. 58).

because prosecutors will find other ways to charge lawyers with misconduct (Ye and Gu 2005).

In the late 2000s, one case that galvanized lawyers across China—even being called "China's trial of the century" (Xu 2010)—was the Li Zhuang case. In 2010, Li Zhuang, a prominent Beijing defense lawyer, was convicted of falsifying evidence and of perjury and was sentenced to two and a half years in prison by a Chongqing lower-level court. The legal community expressed concern about the legality of Li's conviction (Lan 2013, p. 304), which seemed to be closely connected with Bo Xilai's "striking black" campaign underway in Chongqing after 2009.[51] Caught up in the campaign was Gong Gangmo, who had hired Li to defend him. Gong first claimed that the police had tortured him, and after he recanted, police authorities accused Li of "inciting a client to give false testimony." In January 2010, Li was arraigned, tried and sentenced to 30 months in jail. Li firmly denied his guilt and appealed his conviction. However, during the trial of second instance he unexpectedly declared that he was guilty. Thus, because of his confession, his sentence was reduced to eighteen months. Some months before his release in April 2011, prosecutors brought further charges that were later dropped because of lack of evidence.

The case against Li was widely regarded by China's legal community as a travesty of justice and a significant challenge to the survival of their profession. It spurred intense strategic reflections, as it brought into the open how easily the law could be manipulated to serve the interests of the most powerful in society against the principle of the rule of law (Lan 2013). The Chinese media reported widely on the case. *Caixin News*, for example, devoted a cover story and an editorial to it; several websites presented minute-by-minute coverage of the case.[52] Lawyers contend that this case, like many other cases of harassment, detention, and criminal conviction of them merely for doing their job, has had a chilling effect on lawyers in China, highlighting that criminal defense work there is a "high-risk" activity (Guo 2009; Human Rights Watch 2008; Liu and Halliday 2016; Tian 2007, p. 208).

Although Article 306 has not been repealed or amended, under Xi Jinping coverage about it has faded from the headlines. This is because the measures employed to silence the legal profession have expanded as the government has become more brazen in its repression of outspoken defense lawyers. Since

51 The campaign was launched in 2009 by Bo Xilai and his security forces in Chongqing. Thousands alleged criminals were rounded up and tried for crimes including accepting bribes, other forms of economic crime, assault and murder (Trevaskes 2012, p. 65).

52 For a detailed account on the case and coverage by Chinese media, see Liu and Halliday 2016, pp. 122–43.

2015, international scholars have shown increasing concern over the plight of criminal defense lawyers and have followed with dismay the vicissitudes of China's legal profession. Overall, their analysis of the difficulties of criminal defense lawyers can be broadly divided into two main scholarly categories. The first is study of the role of lawyers in authoritarian contexts and their strategies for activity in a repressive environment (Fu and Cullen 2008, 2011; Halliday and Liu 2007; Liu 2011, 2013; Liu and Halliday 2009, 2011, 2016; Michelson 2006, 2007; Michelson and Liu 2010; Macbean and Nesossi 2015; Pils 2007, 2014). The second is the role of lawyers in ensuring the protection of criminal suspects and defendants' rights to both a fair trial and access to justice (Fu 2009; Liang and He 2014; Lu and Miethe 2002; Nesossi 2012, 2013). Scholarly attention has increased in the Xi era because of the concerted attack by authorities on criminal defense lawyers who are willing to provide what the authorities see as an overly vigorous defense of their clients, with many of these lawyers subjected to political persecution through detention, arrest, torture, and criminal conviction. Cases of lawyers caught up in the July 2015 crackdown have been widely covered in Western media, and published scholarly views reflect on both the continuing authoritarian nature of the Chinese government and the relative weakness of the legal profession in China (China Human Rights Lawyers Concern Group 2017; Fu 2017; Gan 2017; Pils 2017).

4 Conclusion

This review of the literature on Chinese procedural justice studies concludes that in China a symbiotic relationship has emerged between criminal justice—criminal laws and institutions—and the party's governance platforms. Scholars in this field understand that legal practices and political narratives go hand in hand, as both help to shape and sustain a particular agenda for China's modernization. Although this has always been the case in post-Mao China, the Xi Jinping administration has made this relationship between narrative and practice even more transparent and explicit. This is because the Xi leadership has transformed *yifa zhiguo*—that is, governing the nation in accordance with the law—into the backbone of the party's governance platform and has promoted procedural justice as a key politicolegal value.

The trends identified in this article regarding synergies between criminal justice policies and Xi's *yifa zhiguo* party governance platform have only become more pronounced since the nineteenth party congress in late 2017, when the CCP announced that the phrase "the party leads over everything" (*dang shi lingdao yiqie de* 党是领导一切的) would be inserted in the party constitution. State constitutional changes passed at the March 2018 National People's Congress (NPC) reflect this vision. The state constitution was amended to create a legal reality for some major changes in the party-state structure, including the creation of a new party-state hybrid, the National Supervision Commission (NSC; Zhonghua renmin gongheguo guojia jiancha weiyuanhui 中华人民共和国国家监察委员会). On March 21, one day after the closing of the March NPC, came the announcement that a number of China's key state organs would be merged with or subsumed under party departments.[53] The party articulates these changes as part of a "new-type party political system" (*xinxing dangzheng zhidu* 新型政党制度). The essence of this type of party political system is the idea that party leadership itself—through codification of its supremacy in the constitution—is the core means of accountability in government and in the judicial system.

The new-type of party political system centers on the idea that strong centralized party leadership provides the most effective means of government accountability. This is a direct repudiation of the Western separation-of-powers idea that dispersed power provides the best system of accountability. As noted earlier, when Xi came to power in late 2012, the political rhetoric in China changed from stability maintenance to rule-of-law thinking, including overtures about procedural propriety, transparency, and preventing miscarriages of justice. Over the past five years, the Xi leadership has progressively built on its initial emphasis on enhancing proceduralism and building accountability. Retreating from Hu Jintao's Harmonious Society—Stability Maintenance governance platform, the new leadership put renewed emphasis on the concept of governing the nation in accordance with the law, or *yifa zhiguo*. This choice was dictated by a perceived need to win back public trust in the politicolegal system and to re-establish public trust in legal institutions and the public legitimacy that had been partially lost during the Hu era. The Xi leadership has sought to foster stronger oversight of political and judicial authorities at the local level, promoting transparency in the justice system and legislating for the prevention of miscarriages of justice. In practice, this has meant a new emphasis on the trial—"putting the trial at the center of the criminal process" or "trial centeredness."

At the beginning of the Xi era, many China observers and legal scholars whose work we have cited here anticipated that a renewed emphasis on *yifa zhiguo* might cause an overhaul of past legal practice. In 2012–2013, scholars pondered the potential utility of the *yifa zhiguo* platform to bring about

53 For an outline of these changes see http://www.gov.cn/zhengce/2018-03/21/content_5276191.htm#1/.

meaningful institutional accountability reforms and whether a new emphasis on procedural justice might improve the prospects for fair trial guarantees in the criminal process. Since that time, the logic behind Xi's *yifa zhiguo* governance platform has unfolded gradually, to reveal the political intentions behind the utility of using *yifa zhiguo* as a central platform. It is now clear that the intent behind Xi's *yifa zhiguo* is to strengthen party leadership through the use of law, to further merge party and state.

Scholars have highlighted an accentuation of coercion and accountability promoted under the banner of *yifa zhiguo*. Regular crackdowns on various social constituencies—human rights lawyers, civil society organizations, and corrupt officials, for example—have been accompanied by reforms in the justice system aimed at curbing police malpractice and judicial corruption that, in the past, had led to miscarriages of justice and abuses of individual rights. These apparently contradictory agendas promoted under the broader umbrella of *yifa zhiguo* have made it clear that the aim of Xi's governance platform is to rebalance the accountability—coercion equation—not by increasing accountability at the expenses of coercion but by intensifying both. Thus, on the whole, Xi's *yifa zhiguo* has provided us with the opportunity to reflect on how his and previous political leaderships have articulated the accountability—coercion relationship and its impact on criminal justice practice.

Central to our review is how scholars have addressed the concept of a fair trial and how it is conceptualized in the Chinese context to serve specific political agendas cast as beneficial for society. Legislators have never advanced due process provisions as discrete legal principles; rather, they have always been linked or subordinated to rules of substantive justice to serve the overall goal of advancing socialist modernization. Indeed, in contrast to Anglo-American conceptions of a fair trial, in China such a guarantee is related only indirectly to protecting the human rights of criminal suspects, defendants, and offenders—and those who work on their behalf. In other words, the protection of individual human rights is but the byproduct of measures that help guarantee procedural fairness; it is not the primary aim or objective of delivering a fair trial. The failure to ratify the ICCPR (signed in 1997) only illustrates this point. The purpose of ensuring fairness in criminal trials is to enhance "judicial justice and efficiency" for the overall purpose of obtaining good substantive outcomes that support the overarching reform goals of state modernization and development. For this reason, as Chinese scholars have highlighted, procedural justice guarantees have remained aspirational and difficult to apply. Vague provisions leave room for contingent and individualized methods of obtaining justice and do not provide remedies for abuses.

In China, party leaders have long argued that the structure of the criminal process needs to reflect basic fairness principles that protect "the people's" interests as a whole. Fairness principles are therefore circumscribed within the overall guiding ideology and policies of the party, whose interests are, the party claims, the very manifestation of those of the people. Therefore, unsurprisingly, China's CPL closely aligns with two key characteristics of Damaška's policy-implementing ideal type. The first is that the trial is essentially an inquiry, with the object of the inquiry (the defendant) being primarily a supplier of information. The second is that the status and role of parties in court debate are determined largely by the trial's "policy-implementing" goal. The characteristics of this ideal model align closely with the stated relationship between the police, the procuratorate, and the courts in China. This close relationship is enabled by a principle in the CPL known as mutual coordination and mutual restraint. Mutual coordination among these three arms affects a defendant's prospects for a fair trial at a number of critical junctures in the trial decision-making process. For instance, judges rely heavily, if not exclusively, on the police's case file containing written statements. Indeed, it is widely acknowledged that the justice system's numerous and wide-ranging miscarriages of justice are overwhelmingly and directly linked to evidentiary factors at the investigation stage, namely, the prevalence of coerced confessions. Although the Xi leadership has put a spotlight on the problem of miscarriages of justice and has enhanced (albeit in a limited way) measures for judicial and police responsibility for misjudged cases, they have done nothing to change the structures of the criminal process that promote the dominance of mutual coordination. Tinkering around the edges of procedural reform through the promotion of trial centeredness has not resulted in any major amendments to the CPL or in any improvement in the protection of the right to a fair trial.

In the Xi era, procedural justice as conceived in socialist ideology is not an instrument aimed at equalizing competing views and political and economic interests in society. Party authorities do not portray it as a tool that can be used to limit political power and ensure party accountability to society at large. This is because, in the party's view, the party and the broad masses of the people have a shared view of fairness and uphold the same interests, since the party's interests are the very manifestation of those of the people. As we highlighted in Part 2 of this article, this understanding of state—society relations aligns with a "corporatist" vision of the state that emphasizes the existence of an organic whole comprising civil society and the state. Inevitably, therefore, judicial independence and structures for external supervision are alien to such a system. As explained in Part 3, this understanding of institutional structures determines the ways in which a criminal trial is conducted and the eventual realization of due process. It is a trial at which lawyers are frequently absent, because they are still seen as outsiders to the system. It is a trial where judicial power is very limited in comparison to the power of the executive, and it provides the police with incentives for closing cases pretrial, too often through coercive means. As Chinese legal scholars acknowledge, this explains the continuing strong emphasis on oral confessions, which many still consider the "king of evidence." Such an emphasis aligns with a traditional inclination in the Chinese criminal justice system toward the presumption of guilt and with a weak evidentiary system still focused on a written case file that is compiled pretrial.

In China today, more than ever before, the party perceives the need to control the discursive space in which issues of justice are discussed and debated. This level of control is made possible by maintaining constant coercive pressure on social forces that seek an alternative vision of government accountability. Rather than shifting its objectives to fair trial guarantees that base accountability on the idea of dispersed power arrangements through independent checks and balances, procedural propriety rests largely on supervisory and accountability measures under more concentrated party rule. Thus, when the Xi administration claims willingness to solve criminal justice problems—interrogational torture, for example—it is not doing so by creating independent exercise of checks and balances or by significantly amending the CPL. Instead, it is profferring enhanced centralized party-led supervision, thus further concerntating power rather than dispersing it.

The Xi leadership deems performance legitimacy as crucial to the goal of party rejuvenation, hence the strong link between the general character of Xi's concentrated political authority and the character of procedural design in the justice system. Of utmost importance to Xi, the party's leadership, and the party at large is not merely the preservation of the political status quo but the rejuvenation of the party's authority and legitimacy so that it can be seen as ruling over everything effectively.

References

Alford, William. 1996. "Tasselled Loafers for Barefoot Lawyers: Transformation and Tension in the World of Chinese Legal Workers." *In China's Legal Reforms*, ed. Stanley Lubman, pp. 22–38. Oxford: Oxford University Press.

Bai Quanmin 白全民 and Cheng Mengqi 承蒙起. 2008. "Xin lüshi fa du jiansuo jiancha gongzuo de wu da yaoqiu 新律师法对监所检察工作的五大要求 [The Five Main

Requirements Imposed by the New Lawyers Law on the Work of the Procuratorate in Detention].” *Jiancha ribao* 检察日报 [*Procuratorial Daily*], April 8: 3.

Bakken, Børge. 2000. *The Exemplary Society: Human Improvement, Social Control and the Dangers of Modernity in China*. New York: Oxford University Press.

Bao Zhenyuan 包振远 and Ma Lifan 马季凡编 eds. 1998. *Zhongguo lidai kuxing shilu* 中国历代酷刑实录 [*Factual Record on Torture in Past Dynasties*]. Beijing: Zhongguo shehui chubanshe.

Baum, Richard. 1986. “Modernisation and Legal Reform in Post-Mao China: The Rebirth of Socialist Legality.” *Studies in Comparative Communism* 19, no. 2: 69–103.

Belkin, Ira. 2011. “China's Tortuous Path toward Ending Torture in Criminal Investigations.” *Columbia Journal of Asian Law* 24, no. 2 (Spring): 273–302.

Belkin, Ira. 2017. “The Chinese Communist Party's Struggle with Public Opinion and the Administration of Criminal Justice.” In *Justice: The China Experience*, eds. Flora Sapio, Susan Trevaskes, Sarah Biddulph and Elisa Nesossi, pp. 195–228. Cambridge: Cambridge University Press.

Benney, Jonathan. 2013. *Defending Rights in Contemporary China*. London: Routledge.

Bian, Jianlin, and Jingjing Li. 2006. “Seeing the Improvement of the Criminal Trial Structure from China's Criminal Courtroom Arrangements (Tribunal Design).” *Frontiers of Law in China* 1, no. 2: 164–84.

Biddulph, Sarah. 2007. *Legal Reform and Administrative Detention Powers in China*. Cambridge: Cambridge University Press.

Biddulph, Sarah. 2015. *The Stability Imperative: Human Rights and Law in China*. Vancouver: UBC Press.

Biddulph, Sarah. 2016. “What to Make of the Abolition of Re-Education through Labour?” In *Legal Reforms and the Deprivation of Liberty in Contemporary China*, eds. Elisa Nesossi, Sarah Biddulph, Flora Sapio, and Susan Trevaskes, pp. 23–42. Abingdon, UK: Routledge.

Biddulph, Sarah. 2017. “Punishments in the Post Re-Education through Labour World: Questions about Minor Crime in China.” In *Chinese Legal Reform and the Global Legal Order: Adoption and Adaptation*, eds. Yun Zhao and Michael Ng, pp. 15–43. Cambridge: Cambridge University Press.

Biddulph, Sarah, Elisa Nesossi, and Susan Trevaskes. 2017a. “Criminal Justice Reform in Xi Jinping's China.” *China Law and Society Review*, no. 2: 63–128.

Biddulph, Sarah, Elisa Nesossi, Flora Sapio, and Susan Trevaskes. 2017b. “Detention and its Reform in the PRC.” *China Law and Society Review*, no. 2: 1–62.

Bing Lin 兵临. 2011. “Xingsufa xiugai shifang jiji xinhao 刑诉法修改释放积极信号 [Amendment of the Criminal Procedure Law Released Active Signals].” *Renmin ribao* 人民日报 [*People's Daily*], August 16: 9.

Bottomley, Stephen, and Simon Bronitt. 2011. *Law in Context*. 4th ed. Annandale, NSW: Federation Press.

Bottoms, Anthony, and Justice Tankebe. 2012. "Beyond Procedural Justice: A Dialogic Approach to Legitimacy in Criminal Justice." *Journal of Criminal Law and Criminology* 102, no. 1: 119–70.

Brødsgaard, Kjeld Erik, and Nis Grünberg. 2014. "The Fourth Plenum of the CPC Makes an Important Decision on Law Reform in China." *Copenhagen Journal of Asian Studies* 32, no. 2: 122–30.

Bucke, Tom, Robert Street, and David Brown. 2000. *The Right of Silence: The Impact of the Criminal Justice and Public Order Act 1994*. Home Office Research Study, no. 199. London: Home Office.

Cai Yanbin 蔡炎斌. 2000. "Lun xingxun bigong lüjin buzhi de yuanyin ji duice 论刑讯逼供屡禁不止的原因及对策 [Discussion about the Causes Explaining the Difficulties in Prohibiting the Extracting Confession through Torture and Its Countermeasures]." *Hunan gong'an gaodeng zhuanke xuexiao xuebao* 湖南公安高等专科学校学报 [*Journal of Hunan Police Academy*], no 2: 54–57.

Cao Zhihua 曹治华. 2008. "Shilun woguo sixing anjian de zhengming biaozhun 试论我国死刑案件的证明标准 [Debates on the Standard of Proof for Death Penalty Cases in China]." *Zhengfa xuekan* 政法学刊 [*Journal of Political Science and Law*] 26, no. 6: 66–69.

Capowski, John J. 2012. "China's Evidentiary and Procedural Reforms, the Federal Rules of Evidence and the Harmonization of Civil and Common Law." *Texas International Law Journal* 47, no. 3: 455–504.

CCP Central Committee. 2014. *Zhongong zhongyan guanyu quanmian tuijinyifa zhiguo ruogan zhongda wenti de jueding* 中共中央关于全面推进依法治国若干重大问题的决定 [*Central Committee Decision on Some Major Questions in Comprehensively Moving Forward Governing the Nation According to Law*]. Xinhuanet, October 28. http://www.xinhuanet.com/politics/2014-10/28/c_1113015372.htm (English translation at https://chinacopyrightandmedia.wordpress.com/2014/10/28/ccp-central-committee-decision-concerning-some-major-questions-in-comprehensively-moving-governing-the-country-according-to-the-law-forward/).

Chen, Albert H.Y. 2016. "China's Long March towards Rule of Law or China's Turn against the Law?" *Chinese Journal of Comparative Law* 4, no. 1: 1–35.

Chen Guangzhong 陈光中. 1998. *Lianheguo xingshi sifa zhunze he Zhongguo xingshi fazhi* 联合国刑事司法准则和中国刑事法制 [*The United Nations Standards and China's Criminal Justice System*]. Beijing: Falü chubanshe.

Chen Guangzhong 陈光中. 2002. *Chenmo quan wenti yanjiu: jianlun ruhe ezhi xingxun bigong* 沉默权问题研究: 兼论如何遏制刑讯逼供 [*Research on the Issue of the Right of Silence: together with a Discussion on How to Extirpate the Extraction of Confession through Torture*]. Beijing: Zhongguo renmin gong'an daxue chubanshe.

Chen Guangzhong 陈光中. 2004. *Zhonghua renmin gongheguo xingshi susongfa zai xiugai zhuanjia jianyigao yu lunzheng* 中华人民共和国刑事诉讼法再修改专家建议

稿与论证 [*The Expert Recommended Draft of the PRC Criminal Procedure Law and Its Reasoning*]. Beijing: Zhongguo fazhi chubanshe.

Chen Guangzhong 陈光中. 2007. "Jianchi chengxu gongzheng yu shiti gongzheng bingzhong zhi wojian: yi xingshi sifa wei shijiao 坚持程序公正与实体公正并重之我见: 以刑事司法为视角 [On Emphasizing Both Procedural Justice and Substantive Justice: As Viewed from the Criminal Prodedure]." *Guojia jianchaguan xueyuan xuebao* 国家检察官学院学报 [*Journal of National Prosecutor's College*] 15, no. 2: 3–6.

Chen Guangzhong 陈光中. 2010. "Xingshi zhengju zhidu gaige ruogan lilun yu shijian wenti zhi tantao—liangyuan sanbu liangge zhengju guiding zhi gongbu wei shijiao 刑事证据制度改革若干理论与实践问题之探讨—两院三部《两个证据规定》之公布为视角 [Research on Several Theoretical and Practical Issues of Criminal Evidential System Reform]." *Zhongguo faxue* 中国法学 [*Chinese Legal Science*], Issue 6: 5–16.

Chen Guangzhong 陈光中 and Guo Zhiyuan 郭志媛. 2014. "Feifa zhengju paichu guize shishi ruogan wenti yanjiu 非法证据排除规则实施若干问题研究 [Research on the Various Problems Concerning the Application of Exclusionary Rules]." *Faxue zazhi* 法学杂志 [*Legal Science Magazine*] Issue 9: 1–16.

Chen, Guangzhong, and Mei Liu. 2007. "Reform of Criminal Evidence System in China." Paper presented at the 20th Anniversary Conference of the International Society for the Reform of Criminal Law (1987–2007)—Twenty Years of Criminal Justice Reform: Past Achievements and Future Challenges, Vancouver, Canada, June.

Chen Guangzhong 陈光中 and Yu Zengzun 于增尊. 2014. "Yanfang yuan'an ruogan wenti sikao 严防冤案若干问题思考 [Consideration on Some Problems in Preventing Wrongful Convictions]." *Faxuejia* 法学家 [*The Jurist*], no. 1: 56–66.

Chen Guangzhong 陈光中, Fan Chongyi 樊崇义, Chen Guoqing 陈国庆, Zhang Xiangjun 张相军, Miao Shengming 苗生明, Wang Xinhuan 王新环, Zou Kaihong 邹开红, Zhang Zhiming 张志铭, Yang Chunlei 杨春雷 and Bian Jianlin 卞建林. 2016. "'Yishenpan wei zhongxin' yu jiancha gongzuo 以审判为中心与检查工作 ['Making the Trial Central to the Process' and Prosecution Work]." *Guojia jianchaguan xueyuan xuebao* 国家检察官学院学报 [*Journal of National Prosecutors College*], no. 1: 7–32.

Chen Guangzhong 陈光中, Zhang Jiahua 张佳华 and Xiao Peiquan 肖沛权. 2013. "Lun wuzui tuiding yuanze jiqi zai Zhongguo de shiyong 论无罪推定原则及其在中国的适用 [Presumption of Innocence and Its Application in China]." *Faxue zazhi* 法学杂志 [*Legal Science Magazine*] 10: 1–8.

Chen Guoqiang 陈国庆 and Zhou Ying 周颖. 2016. "'Yishenpan wei zhongxin' yu jiancha gongzuo 以审判为中心与检查工作 ['Making the Trial Central to the Process' and Prosecution Work]." *Xingshi sifa zhinan* 刑事司法指南 [*Directions in Criminal Justice*], October 14. http://www.jcrb.com/procuratorate/theories/practice/201610/t20161014_1660326.html.

Chen Hu 陈虎. 2010. "Yong chengxu zhengyi zhongjie xingshi yuanjia cuo'an 用程序正义终结刑事冤假错案 [Ending Miscarriages of Justice through Procedural Justice]." *Guangming ribao* 光民日报, June 10. http: http://theory.people.com.cn/GB/11836407.html.

Chen, Jianfu. 2013. *Criminal Law and Criminal Procedure Law in the People's Republic of China*. Leiden: Martinus Nijhoff.

Chen, Jianfu. 2016a. "Efforts towards Procedural Justice in Post-Mao China." In *China's Socialist Rule of Law Reforms under Xi Jinping*, ed. John Garrick and Yan Chang Benne, pp. 94–108. London: Routledge.

Chen, Jianfu. 2016b. "Out of the Shadows and Back to the Future: CPC and the Law in China." *Asia-Pacific Law Review* 24, no. 2: 176–201.

Chen Ruchao 陈如超. 2014. "Xingxun bigong de guojia zhili: 1979–2013 刑讯逼供的国家治理: 1979–2013 [The State Administration of Extraction of Confession through Torture: 1979–2013]." *Zhongguo faxue* 中国法学 [*Chinese Legal Science*], no. 5: 5–25.

Chen Ruihua 陈瑞华. 2008. "Xiang shei bianhu, shei lai qingting? 向谁辩护谁来倾听? [Whose Defense and Who Is Going to Listen?]." In *Xingshi bianhu yu feifa zhengju paichu* 刑事辩护与非法证据排除 [*Defense System and Exclusionary Rules of Illegally Obtained Evidence*], ed. Lang Sheng 郎胜, pp. 69–90. Beijing: Beijing daxue chubanshe.

Chen Ruihua 陈瑞华. "Zhao Zuohaimen hui shao ma? 赵作海们会少吗？ [Can We Get Fewer Zhao Zuohais?]." *Nanfang zhoumo* 南方周末 [Southern Weekend], June 3. http://news.163.com/10/0603/11/688JE7M600014AEE.html.

Chen, Ruihua. 2011. "Initial Research on the Malfunctions of the Criminal Process." *Pacific Rim Law and Policy Journal* 20, no. 2: 359–97.

Chen Ruihua 陈瑞华. 2014. "Xingshi zhengming biaozhun zhong zhukeguan yaosu de guanxi 刑事证明标准中主客观要素的关系 [The Relation between Subjective and Objective Elements in Criminal Proof Standard]." *Zhongguo faxue* 中国法学 [*Chinese Legal Science*], no. 3: 177–95.

Chen Ruihua 陈瑞华. 2016. "Xin jianjie shenli zhuyi: 'tingshen zhongxin zhuyi gaige' de zhuyao zhang'ai 新间接审理主义—庭审中心主义改革的主要障碍 [The New Trial Ideology: The Main Bulwarks to Trial-Centeredness Reform]." *Zhongwai faxue* 中外法学 [*Peking University Law Journal*] 28, no. 4: 845–64.

Chen Ruihua 陈瑞华. 2017. "'Shenpan zhongxin zhuyi gaige' de lilun fansi 审判中心主义改革的理论反思 [Theoretical Reflections on 'Trial Centeredness' Reform]. *Suzhou daxue xuebao (zhexue shehui kexue ban)* 苏州大学学报(哲学社会科学版) [*Journal of Soochow University (Philosophy and Social Science Edition)*], no. 1: 34–43.

Chen, Weidong. 2006. "The Basic Concepts of Re-Modifying the Criminal Procedure Law." *Frontiers of Law in China* 2, no. 1: 153–63.

Chen Weidong 陈卫东. 2016a. "'Yishenpan wei zhongxin': jiedu, shixian yu zhanwang 以审判为中心: 解读、实现与展望 ['Making the Trial Central to the Process':

Interpretation, Realization, and Prospects]. *Dangdai faxue* 当代法学 [*Contemporary Law Review*], Issue 4: 14–21.

Chen Weidong 陈卫东. 2016b. "Yishenpan wei zhongxin: dangdai Zhongguo xingshi sifa gaige de jidian 以审判为中心: 当代中国刑事司法改革的基点 [Making the Trial Central to the Process: The Starting Point of Criminal Justice Reform in Contemporary China]." *Faxuejia* 法学家 [*The Jurist*], no. 4: 1–15.

Chen, Weidong and Taru Spronken, eds. 2012. *Three Approaches to Combating Torture in China*. Maastricht: Intersentia.

Chen Weidong 陈卫东 and Xu Kun 许坤, eds. 2008. *Guifan quzheng xingwei, ezhi xingxun bigong: jingcha peixun shouce* 规范取证行为、遏制刑讯逼供: 警察培训手册 [*Discipline the Practice of Taking Evidence, and Prohibiting the Extraction of Confession through Torture: The Handbook for Training Policemen*]. Beijing: Beijing daxue chubanshe.

Chen Wengeng 陈文锋 and Mo Xiaosong 莫小松. 2008. "Ting shen hou zhengren, bianhu lüshi xianhou bei bu 庭审后证人、辩护律师先后被捕 [After the Trial, First the Witnesses and Then the Defense Lawyer Have Been Arrested]." *Fazhi ribao* 法制日报 [*Legal Daily*], April 26: 6.

Chen Wenqi 陈文奇. 1993. *Zhizhi xingxunbigong bidu* 制止刑讯逼必读 [*The Essence of Prohibiting Extraction of Confession through Torture*]. Taiyuan: Shanxi renmin chubanshe.

Chen, Xi. 2012. *Social Protest and Contentious Authoritarianism in China*. New York: Cambridge University Press.

Chen Yunsheng 陈云生. 2000. *Fan kuxing: dangdai Zhongguo de fazhi he renquan baohu* 反酷刑: 当代中国的法治和人权保护 [*Combating Torture: The Legal System and the Protection of Human Rights in Contemporary China*]. Beijing: Shehui kexue wenxian chubanshe.

Cheng Lei 程雷. 2008. "Ruhe lijie 'lüshi huijian bu bei jianting' 如何理解律师会见不被监听 [How to Interpret 'Lawyers Shall Not Be under Surveillance']." *Jiancha ribao* 检察日报 [*Procuratorial Daily*], January 14: 3.

Cheng Tao 程滔. 2006. *Bianhu lüshi de susong quanli yanjiu* 辩护律师的诉讼权利研究 [*Research on the Procedural Rights of Defense Lawyers*]. Beijing: Zhongguo renmin gong'an daxue chubanshe.

China Human Rights Lawyers Concern Group. 2017. "Torture and Other Cruel, Inhuman or Degrading Treatments in the 709 Crackdown: A Summary of Cases." July 9. http://www.chrlawyers.hk/sites/default/files/20170709%20-%20Torture%20in%20the%20709%20Crackdown%20%28ENG%29.pdf.

China Radio International. 2012. "Zhongguo de sifa gongzheng wangluo fangtan 中国的司法公正网络访谈 [Online Forum on Chinese Judicial Justice]." November 13. http://gb.cri.cn/news/other/18da/shibada2012111301.htm.

Clarke, Donald. 2003. "Puzzling Observations in Chinese Law: When Is a Riddle Just a Mistake?" In *Understanding China's Legal System: Essays in Honour of Jerome A. Cohen*, ed. C. Stephen Hsu, pp. 93–121. New York: New York University Press.

Clarke, Donald. 2015. "China's Legal System and the Fourth Plenum." *Asia Policy*, Issue 20: 10–16.

Cohen, Jerome. 1968. *The Criminal Process in the People's Republic of China, 1949–63: An Introduction*. Cambridge, MA: Harvard University Press.

Conner, Alison. 1994. "Lawyers and Legal Professionals during the Republican Period." In *Civil Law in Qing and Republican China*, eds. Kathryn Bernhardt and Philip C.C. Huang, pp. 215–48. Stanford: Stanford University Press.

CPLC [Central Political-Legal Committee 中共中央政法委]. 2013. "Zhongyang zhengfawei guanyu qieshi fangzhi yuanjia cuo'an de guiding 中央政法委关于切实防止冤假错案的规定 [CPC Political-Legal Committee Provisions on Preventing Miscarriage of Justice]." Zhongzhengwei 中政委 [CPC Political-Legal Committee], no. 27 (March 2). http://blog.sina.com.cn/s/blog_60d9a2d60101qrdn.html.

Creemers, Rogier. 2015. "China's Constitutionalism Debate: Content, Context and Implications." *The China Journal* 74: 91–109.

Cui Min 崔敏. 2002. "Zai lun ezhi xingxun bigong 再论遏制刑讯逼供 [A Rediscussion on Combating Torture]." In *Chenmo quan wenti yanjiu: jianlun ruhe ezhi xingxun bigong* 沉默权问题研究。兼论如何遏制刑讯逼供 [*Research on the Issue of the Right to Silence: A Discussion on Ways to Limit Extraction of Confession through Torture*], ed. Chen Guangzhong 陈光中, pp. 332–48. Beijing: Zhongguo renmin gong'an daxue chubanshe.

Cui Min 崔敏. 2009. *Xingsshi susong yu zhengju yunyong* 刑事诉讼与证据运用 [*Criminal Litigation and the Use of Evidence*]. Beijing: Zhongguo renmin gong'an daxue chubanshe.

Dai, Yuzhong. 2010. "The Pursuit of Criminal Justice." In *China's Journey Toward the Rule of Law: Legal Reform, 1978–2008*, eds. Cai Dingjian and Wang Chenguang, pp. 155–97. Leiden: Brill.

Damaška, Mirjan. 1986. *The Faces of Justice and State Authority: A Comparative Approach to the Legal Process*. New Haven/London: Yale University Press.

Dang Jiangzhou 党江舟. 2005. *Zhongguo songshi wenhua: gudai lüshi xianxiang de jiedu* 中国讼师文化: 古代律师现象解读 [*The Culture of Litigation Masters in China: Interpretations on the Phenomenon of Ancient Lawyers*]. Beijing: Beijing daxue chubanshe.

Daum, Jeremy. 2011. "Tortuous Progress: Early Cases under China's New Procedures for Excluding Evidence in Criminal Cases." *International Law and Politics* 43: 699–712.

Daum, Jeremy. 2014. "Judicial Independence, Transparency and Accountability." China Law Translate. https://www.chinalawtranslate.com/judicial-independence-transparency-and-accountability/?lang=en/.

Daum, Jeremy. 2017. "Why China's Exclusionary Rules Won't Stop Police Torture." Blog post. July 1. http://www.chinalawtranslate.com/8481-2/?lang=en/.

deLisle, Jacques. 2017. "Law in the China Model 2.0: Legality, Developmentalism and Leninism under Xi Jinping." *Journal of Contemporary China* 26, no. 103: 68–84.

Deng Kezhu 邓克珠 and Wang Chaohui 王朝晖. 2003. "Xingfa di 306 tiao yu lüshi de quanli 刑法第 306 条与律师的权利 [Article 306 of the Criminal Law and the Rights of Lawyers]." *Zhongguo lüshi* 中国律师 [*Chinese Lawyers*] 4: pp. 37–39.

Ding, Xiaodong. 2017. "Law According to the Communist Party of China: Constitutionalism and Socialist Rule of Law." *Modern China* 43, no. 3: 322–52.

Du Bai 独白. 2002. "Zhongguo lüshi: bei wuru de yu bei sunhai de 中国律师: 被侮辱的和被损害的 [Chinese Lawyers: Insulted and Wounded]." *Fazhi yu jingji* 法制与经济 [*The Legal System and the Economy*] Issue 5: 59–62.

Dutton, Michael. 2005. *Policing Chinese Politics: A History*. Durham: Duke University Press.

Fan Chongyi 樊崇义. 1997. "Jianlun zhengju buzu, zhikong de fanzui bu neng chengli de wuzui panjue 简论证据不足，指控的犯罪不能成立的无罪判决之适用 [Brief on Application of Acquittal Sentence due to Not Being Able to Establish Charged Crime Based on Insufficient Evidence]." *Zhengfa luntan* 政法论坛 [*Tribune of Political Science and Law*], no. 3: 57–61.

Fan Chongyi 樊崇义. 2007. *Xingshi susongfa zai xiugai lixing sikao* 刑事诉讼法再修改理性思考 [*Rational Thinking on the Amendment of the Criminal Procedure Law*]. Beijing: Zhongguo renmin gong'an daxue chubanshe.

Fan Chongyi 樊崇义. 2016. "Xingshi zhengju guize lifa jianyi baogao 刑事证据规则立法建议报告 [Legislative Proposal Report on the Rules of Criminal Evidence]." *Zhongwai faxue* 中外法学 [*Peking University Law Journal*], no. 2: 285–315.

Fan Chongyi 樊崇义, ed. 2005. *Xingshi shenqian chengxu gaige yu zhanwang* 刑事审前程序改革与展望 [*Reform and Perspectives on Criminal Pretrial Procedures*]. Beijing: Zhongguo renmin gong'an daxue chubanshe.

Fan Chongyi 樊崇义 and Gu Yongzhong 顾永忠. 2007. *Zhencha xunwen chengxu gaige shizheng yanjiu* 侦查讯问程序改革实证研究 [*Positive Research on the Reform of Interrogation Procedures*]. Beijing: Zhongguo renmin gong'an daxue chubanshe.

Fang Baoguo 房保国 and Zhang Qingsong 张青松. 2005. "Lüshi huijian nan de xianzhuang yu chulu 律师会见难的现状与出路 [Lawyers' Difficulties in Meeting Their Clients: Present Situation and Solutions]." In *Xingshi bianhu zhidu de shizheng kaocha* 刑事辩护制度的实证考察 [*Empirical Investigation on the System of Criminal Defense*], ed. Chen Ruihua 陈瑞华, pp. 34–62. Beijing: Beijing daxue chubanshe.

Fewsmith, Joseph. 2012. "Social Management as a Way of Coping with Heightened Social Tensions." *China Leadership Monitor* 36. http://media.hoover.org/sites/default/files/documents/CLM36JF.pdf.

Findlay, Mark. 1999. "'Independence' and the Judiciary in the PRC." In *Law, Capitalism and Power in East Asia: The Rule of Law and Legal Institutions*, ed. Kanishka Jayasuriya, pp. 281–99. London: Routledge.

Fiskesjö, Magnus. 2017. "The Return of the Show Trial: China's Televised 'Confessions.'" *Asia-Pacific Journal Japan Focus* 15, no. 13: 1–34. https://apjjf.org/-Magnus-Fiskesj—/5052/article.pdf.

Fiskesjö, Magnus. 2018. "Confessions Made in China." *Made in China* 3, no. 1: 18–22. http://www.chinoiresie.info/PDF/Made-in-China-01-2018.pdf.

Fu, Hualing. 1998. "Criminal Defence in China: The Possible Impact of the 1996 Criminal Procedure Law Reform." *The China Quarterly*, no. 153: 31–48.

Fu, Hualing. 2007. "When Lawyers Are Prosecuted ... the Struggle of a Profession in Transition." *Journal of Comparative Law* 2, no. 2: 95–133.

Fu, Hualing. 2009. "Access to Justice and Constitutionalism in China." In *Building Constitutionalism in China*, eds. Stéphanie Balme and Michael W. Dowdle, pp. 163–78. New York: Palgrave Macmillan.

Fu, Hualing. 2011. "Institutionalizing Criminal Process in China." In *The Development of the Chinese Legal System: Change and Challenges*, ed. Guanghua Yu, pp. 26–48. London: Routledge.

Fu, Hualing. 2013. "Politicized Challenges, Depoliticized Responses: Political Monitoring in China's Transitions." University of Hong Kong Faculty of Law Research Paper no. 2013/014. https://papers.ssrn.com/sol3/papers.cfm?abstract_id=2250073.

Fu, Hualing. 2016. "Between Deference and Defiance: Courts and Penal Populism in Chinese Capital cases." In *The Death Penalty in China: Policy, Practice, and Reform*, eds. Bin Liang and Hong Lu, 274–99. New York: Columbia University Press.

Fu, Hualing. 2017. "What Future Is There for Human Rights Lawyering in China?" *Made in China* 2, no. 2. https://www.chinoiresie.info/what-future-is-there-for-human-rights-lawyering-in-china/.

Fu, Hualing, and Richard Cullen. 2008. "*Weiquan* (Rights Protection) Lawyering in an Authoritarian State: Toward Critical Lawyering." *The China Journal* 59: 111–27.

Fu, Hualing, and Richard Cullen. 2011. "Climbing the *Weiquan* Ladder: A Radicalizing Process for Rights-Protection Lawyers." *The China Quarterly*, no. 205: 40–59.

Fuma, Susumu. 2007. "Litigation Masters and Litigation System of Ming and Qing China." *International Journal of Asian Studies* 4, no. 1: 79–111.

Gan, Nectar. 2017. "Isolated, Tortured, and Mentally Scarred ... The Plight of China's Persecuted Human Rights Lawyers." *South China Morning Post*. July 9. http://www.scmp.com/news/china/policies-politics/article/2101819/chinas-human-rights-lawyers-continue-fight-victims-709/.

Gao Zhiqing 高志卿. 1998. "Xingxun bigong de weihai, chansheng yuanyin ji yufang 刑讯逼供的危害、产生原因及预防 [The Peril, Causes and Prevention of Extraction of Confession through Torture].” *Luoyang shizhuan xuebao* 洛阳师专学报 [*Journal of Luoyang Teachers College*], Issue 6: 30–32.

Gelatt, Timonthy. 1982. “The People’s Republic of China and the Presumption of Innocence.” *Journal of Criminal Law and Criminology* 73, no. 1: 259–316.

Gong Renren 龚刃韧. 2016. “Jinzhi kuxing gongyue zai Zhongguo de shishi wenti 《禁止酷刑公约》在中国的实施问题 [The Problems Concerning the Implementation of Convention against Torture in China].” *Zhongwai faxue* 中外法学 [*Peking University Law Journal*] 28, no. 4: 955–70.

Gu Yongzhong 顾永忠. 2012. “Xingshi susongfa xiugai zhong de lüshi bianhu zhidu 刑事诉讼法修改中的律师辩护制度 [Improvement of Criminal Procedural Law of the Criminal Defense System].” *Zhongguo falü* 中国法律 [*Chinese Law*], Issue 2: 26–27, 82–83.

Guan Yu 管宇. 2008. *Xingshi shenqian chengxu lüshi bianhu* 刑事审前程序律师辩护 [*Criminal Defense during Criminal Pretrial Proceedings*]. Beijing: Falü chubanshe.

Guo Xiaoyu 郭晓宇. 2009. “Si da liyou quxiao ‘lüshi weizheng zui’: Zhang Yan daibiao jianyi feichu xingfa di sanbailiu tiao 四大理由取消律师伪证罪 张燕代表建议废除刑法第三百零六条 [Four Main Reasons for Repealing ‘Lawyers Perjury Crime’: The Representative Zhang Yang Suggests the Abolition of Article 306 of the Criminal Law].” *Fazhi ribao* 法制日报 [*Legal Daily*], March 10.

Guo, Zhiyuan. 2011. *The China Experience: A Survey of Pilot Programs on Criminal Justice Reform*. Beijing: Peking University Press.

Guo, Zhiyuan. 2014. “Criminal Procedure, Law Reform and Stability.” In *The Politics of Law and Stability in China*, eds. Susan Trevaskes, Elisa Nesossi, Sarah Biddulph, and Flora Sapio, 250–87. Cheltenham, UK: Edward Elgar.

Guo Zhiyuan 郭志媛. 2015. “Feifa zhengju paichu fanwei jieding de kunjing yu chulu 非法证据排除范围界定的困境与出路 [Plight and Way out for Exclusionary Rule of Illegally Obtained Confession and a Probe into Reform of Criminal Interrogation].” *Zhengju kexue* 证据科学 [*Evidentiary Science*] 23: 645–52.

Guo, Zhiyuan. 2017. “The First Step of the Long March: Implementing the Exclusionary Rule in China.” *Asia-Pacific Law Review* 25, no. 1: 48–76.

Halliday, Terence C., and Sida Liu. 2007. “Birth of a Liberal Movement? Looking through a One-Way Mirror at Lawyers’ Defense of Criminal Defendants in China.” In *Fighting for Political Freedom: Comparative Studies of the Legal Complex and Political Liberalism*, eds. Terence C. Halliday, Lucien Karpik and Malcolm M. Feeley, pp. 65–108. Oxford: Hart.

Han Xu 韩旭. 2015. “Xin xingshi susongfa shishi yilai lüshi bianhu nan wenti shizheng yanjiu: yi S sheng weili de fenxi 新刑事诉讼法实施以来律师辩护难问题实证研究：以S省为例的分析 [Empirical Research on the Difficulties of Defense Lawyers after the Implementation of the New Criminal Procedure Law: Analysis of S Province as an Example].” *Falü luntan* 法律论坛 [*Legal Forum*] 30, no. 3: 134–41.

He Jiahong 何家弘. 2013. "Shiyong feifa zhengju paichu guize xuyao sifa panli 适用非法证据排除规则需要司法判例 [Judicial Precedents Are Needed for Applying the Exclusionary Rule against Illegally Obtained Evidence]." *Faxuejia* 法学家 [*The Jurist*], Issue 2: 106–18, 179.

He, Jiahong. 2016. *Back from the Dead: Wrongful Convictions and Criminal Justice in China*. Honolulu: University of Hawai'i Press.

He, Jiahong, and Ran He. 2012. "Empirical Studies of Wrongful Convictions in Mainland China." *University of Cincinnati Law Review* 80, no. 4: 1277–92.

He, Ni. 2013. *Chinese Criminal Trials: A Comprehensive Inquiry*. New York: Springer.

He, Xin. 2009. "Court Finance and Court Reactions to Judicial Reforms: A Tale of Two Chinese Courts." *Law and Policy* 31, no. 4: 463–86.

He, Xin. 2012. "Black Hole of Responsibility: The Adjudication Committee's Role in a Chinese Court." *Law and Society Review* 46, no. 4: 681–712.

He, Xin. 2017. "The Politics of Courts in China." *China Law and Society Review* 2, no. 2: 129–53.

Hecht, Jonathan. 1996. *Opening to Reform? An Analysis of China's Revised Criminal Procedure Law*. New York: Lawyers Committee for Human Rights.

Hu Jianpo 胡建泼. 2002. "Shilun jianli woguo de chenmo quan zhidu 试论建立我国的沉默权制度 [On the Establishment of the System of the Right of Silence in China]." In *Chenmo quan wenti yanjiu: Jianlun ruhe ezhi xingxun bigong* 沉默权问题研究—兼论如何遏制刑讯逼供 [*Research on the Issue of the Right of Silence: Together with a Discussion on How to Prohibit the Extraction of Confession through Torture*], ed. Chen Guangzhong 陈光中, pp. 193–225. Beijing: Zhongguo renmin gong'an daxue chubanshe.

Hu Zhifeng 胡志凤. 2017. "Zhencha xunwen luyin luxiang zhidu de shehui pinggu: jishu, guocheng yu wenti daoxiang 侦查讯问录音录像制度的社会评估：技术，过程与问题导向 [Social Assessment of the System of Audiovisual Recording During Criminal Interrogation: Technology, Process and Problem-Oriented]." *Zhongguo xinjing xueyuan xuebao* 中国刑警学院学报 [*Journal of China Criminal Police College*], no. 2: 34–42.

Huang, Shiyuan. 2012. "Chinese Wrongful Convictions: Discovery and Rectification." *University of Cincinnati Law Review* 80, no. 4 (Summer): 1195–218.

Huang Taiyun 黄太云. 1996. "Xingshi susong zhidu de zhongda gaige—Xingshi susongfa xiugai de jige zhongda wenti shuyao 刑事诉讼制度的重大改革: 刑事诉讼法修改的几个重大问题述要 [Critical Reform on Criminal Lawsuit System: Brief on Several Important Topics in Amending Criminal Procedure Law]." *Zhongguo faxue* 中国法学 [*Chinese Legal Science*], Issue 2: 29–39.

Human Rights Watch. 2008. *Walking on Thin Ice. Control, Intimidation and Harassment of Lawyers in China*. New York: Human Rights Watch. https://www.hrw.org/reports/2008/china0408/china0408web.pdf.

Human Rights Watch. 2016. *Special Measures. Detention and Torture in the Chinese Communist Party's Shuanggui System*. New York: Human Rights Watch. https://www.hrw.org/sites/default/files/report_pdf/china1216_web.pdf.

Jayasuriya, Kanishka. 1999a. "Introduction: A Framework for the Analysis of Legal Institutions in East Asia." In *Law, Capitalism and Power in East Asia: The Rule of Law and Legal Institutions*, ed. Kanishka Jayasuriya, pp. 1–27. London: Routledge.

Jayasuriya, Kanishka. 1999b. "Corporatism and Judicial Independence within Statist Legal Institutions in East Asia." In *Law, Capitalism and Power in East Asia: The Rule of Law and Legal Institutions*, ed. Kanishka Jayasuriya, pp. 173–204. London: Routledge.

Jiang, Na. 2013. "Death Penalty Reforms in China: Lessons from Wrongful Convictions?" *Tsinghua China Law Review* 5: 126–50.

Jiang, Na. 2016. *Wrongful Convictions in China: Comparative and Empirical Perspectives*. Berlin: Springer.

Jiang, Su. 2018. "Old Wine in New Bottles? New Strategies for Judicial Accountability in China." *International Journal of Law, Crime and Justice* 52: 74–85.

Jiao Hongyan 焦红艳 and Chen Hongwei 陈虹伟. 2008. "Xingshi bianhu lüshi re pan lüshi fa xingsu fa shixian wu feng duijie 刑事辩护律师热盼律师法刑诉法实现无缝对接 [Criminal Defense Lawyers Fervently Hope that the Lawyers Law and the Criminal Procedure Law Will Be Consistent]." *Fazhi ribao* 法制日报 [*Legal Daily*], February 3: 6.

Jin Liangnian 金良年. 1991. *Kuxing yu Zhongguo shehui* 酷刑与中国社会 [*Torture and Chinese Society*]. Hangzhou: Zhejiang renmin chubanshe.

Jin Xueren 靳学仁. 2007. *Xingxun bigong yanjiu* 刑讯逼供研究 [*Research on the Extraction of Confession through Torture*]. Beijing: Zhongguo jiancha chubanshe.

Johnson, David, and Franklin Zimring. 2009. *The Next Frontier: National Development, Political Change, and the Death Penalty in Asia*. Oxford: Oxford University Press.

Joint Opinion. Zuigao renmin fayuan, zuigao renmin jianchayuan, gong'anbu, guojia anquanbu, sifabu 最高人民法院，最高人民检察院，公安部，国家安全部，司法部 [Supreme People's Court, Supreme People's Procuratorate, Ministry of Public Security, Ministry of National Security, and Ministry of Justice]. 2016. *Guanyu tuijin yishenpan weizhongxin de xingshi susong zhidu gaige de yijian* 关于推进以审判为中心的刑事诉讼制度改革的意见 [*Opinions on Promoting the Reform of The Trial-Centered Criminal Procedural System*]. October 10. http://politics.people.com.cn/n1/2016/1010/c1001-28765885.html.

Karstedt, Susanne. 2013. "Trusting Authorities: Legitimacy, Trust and Collaboration in Non-Democratic Regimes." In *Legitimacy and Criminal Justice*, ed. Justice Tankebe and Alison Liebling, pp. 127–56. Oxford: Oxford University Press.

Keith, Ronald. 1994. *China's Struggle for the Rule of Law*. London: St. Martin's Press.

Keith, Ronald C., and Zhiqiu Lin. 2001. *Law and Justice in China's New Marketplace*. New York: Palgrave.

Keller, Perry. 1994. "Sources of Order in Chinese Law." *American Journal of Comparative Law* 42, no. 4: 711–59.

Krygier, Martin. 2011. "Four Puzzles about the Rule of Law: Why, What, Where? And Who Cares?" *Nomos* 50: 64–104.

Kuang, Kai, and Bin Liang. 2015a. "Criminal Appellants: Claims and Appellate Courts' Answers: An Empirical Analysis of Criminal Appeals in Hunan Province, China." *Australian and New Zealand Journal of Criminology* 48, no. 4: 545–71.

Kuang, Kai, and Bin Liang. 2015b. "Efficiency and Justice and Fairness: An Empirical Analysis of Criminal Appeals in Hunan Province, China." *European Journal of Criminal Policy Research* 21: 565–90.

Lam, Willy. 2009. "The Politicisation of China's Law-Enforcement Apparatus." *China Perspectives* 2: 42–51.

Lan, Rongjie. 2013. "Killing the Lawyer as the Last Resort: The Li Zhuang Case and Its Effects on Criminal Defence in China." In *Comparative Perspectives on Criminal Justice in China*, ed. Mike McConville and Eva Pils, pp. 304–20. Cheltenham, UK: Edward Elgar.

Langford, Ian. 2009. "Fair Trial: The History of an Idea." *Journal of Human Rights* 9, no. 1: 37–52.

Leng, Shao-chuan, and Huangdah Chiu. 1985. *Criminal Justice in Post-Mao China: Analysis and Documents*. Albany: State University of New York Press.

Lewis, Margaret. 2011. "Controlling Abuse to Maintain Control: The Exclusionary Rule in China." *New York University Journal of International Law and Politics* 43, no. 3 (Spring): 629–98.

Lewis, Margaret. 2012. "Presuming Innocence, or Corruption, in China." *Columbia Journal of Transnational Law* 50, no. 2: 287–370.

Lewis, Margaret. 2014. "Criminal Law Pays: Penal Law's Contribution to China's Economic Development." *Vanderbilt Journal of Transnational Law* 47, no. 2: 371–450.

Li, Anthony H.F. 2016. "Centralisation of Power in the Pursuit of Law-Based Governance: Legal Reform under the Xi Administration." *China Perspectives* 2: 63–68.

Li Changsheng 李昌盛. 2012. "Weifa zhencha xingwei de chengxuxing zhicai xiaoguo yanjiu: yi feifa kougong paichu guize wei zhongxin 违法侦查行为的程序性制裁效果研究—以非法口供排除规则为中心 [Effects of Sanctions for Procedural Violations: Focusing on Inadmissibility of Illegally Obtained Oral Evidence]." *Xiandai faxue* 现代法学 [*Modern Law Science*] 34, no. 3: 110–20.

Li Feng 李峰. 2003. "Nuli shijian, zhifa weimin 努力实践执法为民 [Enforcing Laws Diligently for the People]." *Renmin ribao* 人民日报 [*People's Daily*], September 24: 14.

Li Hanjun 李汉军. 2003. "Dangdai Zhongguo de kuxing ji fan kuxing zhuangkuang 当代中国的酷刑及反酷刑状况 [The Current Situation on Torture and Combating Torture in Contemporary China]." In *Kuxin ezhi lun* 酷刑遏制论 [*Discussion on*

Limiting Torture], ed. Zhao Bingzhi 赵秉志编, pp. 113–54. Beijing: Zhongguo renmin gong'an daxue chubanshe.

Li, Hongbing. 2003. "An Investigation of the Case of Zhang Jianzhong." *21st Century Business Herald*, March 12: 6.

Li, Jia, and Wang Zhuhao. 2014. "A Trail to Modernity: Observations on the New Developments of China's Evidence Legislation Movement in a Global Context." *Indiana Journal of Global Legal Studies* 21, no. 2: 683–705.

Li, Li. 2014. *Judicial Discretion within Adjudicative Committee Proceedings in China: A Bounded Rationality Analysis*. Berlin: Springer.

Li Lin 李林. 2015. "Sifa ruhe chengwei zuihou yidao fangxian 司法如何成为最后一道防线 [How Justice Is the Last Line of Defense]." *Qiushi* 求是 [*Seeking Truth*], November 5.

Li, Ling. 2015a. "Chinese Characteristics of the Socialist Rule of Law: Will the Fourth Plenum Cure the Problems of the Chinese Judicial System?" *Asia Policy* 20, no. 1: 17–22.

Li, Ling. 2015b. "'Rule of Law' in a Party-State: A Conceptual Interpretive Framework of the Constitutional Reality of China." *Asian Journal of Law and Society* 2: 93–113.

Li, Ling. 2016. "The Chinese Communist Party and People's Courts: Judicial Dependence in China." *American Journal of Comparative* Law 64, no. 1: 37–74.

Li, Ling. 2017. "Anticorruption Campaign and the Transformation of the Central Commission of Discipline and Inspection in China (2013–2017)." Working paper, Institute of Human Sciences, Vienna.

Li Shuang 李爽. 2016. "Youhua sifa zhiquan peizhi de lilun jieshi yu zhidu jiangou 优化司法职权配置的理论解释与制度建构 [Conceptual Interpretation and Systematic Construction of the Theory behind Optimizing the Allocation of Judicial Authority]." *Fazhi yu shehui fazhan* 法制与社会发展 [*Legal System and Social Development*], no. 2: 58–65.

Li, Victor H. 1977. *Law without Lawyers: A Comparative View of Law in China and the United States*. Boulder: Westview Press.

Li Yao 姚莉. 2003. "Sifa gongzheng yaosu fenxi 司法公正要素分析 [Analysis of Elements of Judicial Justice]." *Faxue yanjiu* 法学研究 [*Legal Research*] 5: 2–23.

Li, Yuwen. 2000. "Lawyers in China: A 'Flourishing' Profession in a Rapidly Changing Society?" *China Perspectives*, Issue 27: 20–39.

Li, Yuwen. 2014. *The Judicial System and Reform in Post-Mao China: Stumbling Towards Justice*. Abington Oxon, UK: Routledge.

Liang, Bin, and Ni He. 2014. "Criminal Defense in Chinese Courtroom: An Empirical Inquiry." *International Journal of Offender Therapy and Comparative Criminology* 58, no. 10: 1230–52.

Liang, Bin, Hong Lu, and Ni He. 2016. "Political Embeddedness and Its Impact on Chinese Criminal Defense Lawyers' Professional Practice: An Empirical Testing." *European Journal on Criminal Policy and Research* 22: 341–61.

Liang, Bin, Ni Phil He, and Hong Lu. 2014. "The Deep Divide in China's Criminal Justice System: Contrasting Perceptions of Lawyers and the Iron Triangle." *Crime, Law and Social Change* 62, no. 5: 585–601.

Liebman, Benjamin L. 2011. "A Populist Threat to China's Courts?" In *Chinese Justice: Civil Dispute Resolution in Contemporary China*, ed. Margaret Y.K. Woo and Mary E. Gallagher, pp. 269–313. Cambridge: Cambridge University Press.

Liebman, Benjamin L. 2015. "Leniency in Chinese Criminal Law? Everyday Justice in Henan." *Berkley Journal of International Law* 33, no. 1: 153–222.

Lin Hua 林华, ed. 1992. *Zhongguo falü jichu* 中国法律基础 [*The Foundations of Chinese Law*]. Guangzhou: Zhongshan daxue chubanshe.

Lin Jingsong 林劲松. 2003. "Lun woguo wuzui tuiding yuanze de fei wanzhengxing 论我国无罪推定原则的非完整性 [On the Incompleteness of Presumption of Innocence in China]." In *Ershiyi Shiji Zhongguo xingshi chengxu gaige yanjiu—Zhonghua Renmin Gongheguo xingshi susong fa di er xiuzheng an xuezhe jianyigao* 世纪中国刑事程序改革研究—中华人民共和国刑事诉讼法第二修正案学者建议稿 [Research on *21st Century China's Criminal Procedure Reform: Second Amendment to the Criminal Procedure Law of the People's Republic of China (Proposal by Scholars)*], ed. Xu Jingcun 徐静村, pp. 227–39. Beijing: Falü chubanshe.

Lin Xin 林欣. 1983. "Wuzui tuiding haishi wuzui jiading? 无罪推定 还是 无罪假定? [Presumption of Innocence or Assumption of Innocence?]." *Zhongguo shehui kexue* 中国社会科学 [*Social Sciences in China*], no. 3: 173–79.

Lin, Zhiqiu. 2016. "Advancements and Controversies in China's Recent Sentencing Reforms." *China Information* 30, no. 3: 357–76.

Lin Zhongliang 林中梁. 2004. *Geji dangwei zhengfawei de zhineng ji hongguan zhengfa gongzuo* 各级党委政法委的职能及宏观政法工作 [*The Functions and Macroscopic Tasks of the Politico-Legal Affairs Work of at All Levels of Party Committee and Politico-Legal Affairs Committees*]. Beijing: Chang'an chubanshe.

Lippke, Richard. 2016. *Taming the Presumption of Innocence*. Oxford: Oxford University Press.

Liu, Caiyu. 2017. "Top Justice Warns against 'Western Trap' of Judicial Independence." *Global Times*, January 15. http://www.globaltimes.cn/content/1028952.shtml.

Liu Hongjun 刘洪军. 1997. "Lüshi huijian: rang wo xihuan rang wo you 律师会见：让我喜欢让我忧 [Lawyers' Meetings: I Like It and I Am Worried about It]." *Zhongguo lüshi* [*Chinese Lawyer*], Issue 7: 45.

Liu Jinlin 刘金林. 2008. "Xiugai lüshi fa jiu dengyu xiugai xingshi susong fa 修改律师法就等于修改刑事诉讼法 [Amending the Lawyers Law is Tantamount to Amending the Criminal Procedure Law]." *Jiancha ribao* 检察日报 [*Procuratorial Daily*], April 6: 3.

Liu Sida 刘思达. 2007. *Shiluo de chengbang: dangdai Zhongguo falü zhiye bianqian* 失落的城: 当代中国法律职业变迁 [*The Lost Polis: Transformation of the Legal Profession in Contemporary China*]. Beijing: Beijing daxue chubanshe.

Liu Sida 刘思达. 2011. "Lawyers, State Officials, and Significant Others: Symbiotic Exchange in the Chinese Legal Services Market." *The China Quarterly*, no. 206: 276–93.

Liu Sida 刘思达. 2013. "Falü zhiye de zhengzhi mingyun 法律职业的政治命运 [The Political Fate of the Legal Profession]." *Jiaoda faxue* 交大法学 [*Shanghai Jiaotong University Law Review*], no. 1: 93–100.

Liu, Sida, and Terence C. Halliday. 2009. "Recursivity in Legal Change: Lawyers and Reforms of China's Criminal Procedure Law." *Law and Social Inquiry* 34, no. 4: 911–50.

Liu, Sida, and Terence C. Halliday. 2011. "Political Liberalism and Political Embeddedness: Understanding Politics in the Work of Chinese Criminal Defence Lawyers." *Law and Society Review* 45, no. 4: 831–65.

Liu, Sida, and Terence C. Halliday. 2016. *Criminal Defense in China: The Politics of Lawyers at Work*. Cambridge: Cambridge University Press.

Liu, Sida, and Zhizhou Wang. 2015. "The Fall and Rise of Law and Social Science in China." *Annual Review of Law and Social Science*, no. 11: 373–94.

Liu Wenyuan 刘文元. 2003. *Lüshi weiquan anli xuan* 律师维权案例选 [*Selection of Cases of Right Defense Lawyers*]. Changchun: Jilin renmin chubanshe.

Liu Zhiwei 刘志伟, Wang Zhenxiang 王珍祥 and Zhang Li 张莉. 2007. "Zhencha jiandu zhong de lüshi zuoyong 侦查监督中的律师作用 [The Importance of Lawyers to Supervise Investigations]." In *Lüshi bianhu zhidu yanjiu: yi shenqian chengxu zhong de lüshi zuoyong wei shijiao* 律师辩护制度研究—以审前程序中的律师作用为视角 [*Study on Lawyer Defense System: A Perspective on the Role of Defense Lawyers in Pretrial Procedures*], eds. Shi Shaoxia 石少侠 and Xu Henan 徐鹤喃, pp. 96–101. Beijing: Zhongguo jiancha chubanshe.

Lo, Carlos Wing-hung. 1995. *China's Legal Awakening: Legal Theory and Criminal Justice in Deng's China*. Hong Kong: Hong Kong University Press.

Long Zongzhi 龙宗智. 2004. "Paihuai yu chuantong yu xiandai zhijian: Lun Zhongguo xingshi susongfa de zai xiugai 徘徊于传统与现代之间: 论中国刑事诉讼法的再修改 [Wandering between Tradition and Contemporary: Discussion on the Second Amendment of the Criminal Procedure Law of the PRC]." *Zhengfa luntan* 政法论坛 [*Tribune of Political Science and Law*], no. 5: 81–93.

Long Zongzhi 龙宗智. 2010. "Liangge zhengju guiding de guifan yu zhixing ruogan wenti yanjiu 两个证据规定的规范与执行若干问题研究 [Research on Two Evidential Regulations' Norms and Applications]." *Zhongguo faxue* 中国法学 [*Chinese Legal Science*], Issue 6: 17–32.

Long, Zongzhi. 2014. "'Beyond Reasonable Doubt' in the Chinese Legal Context." *Peking University Law Journal* 1, no. 2: 339–71.

Long Zongzhi 龙宗智. 2015. "'Yishenpan wei zhongxin' de gaige jiqi xiandu 以审判为中心的改革及其限度 [Reforms and Limitations of 'Making the Trial Central to the Process]." *Zhongwai faxue* 中外法学 [*Peking University Law Journal*], no. 4: 846–60.

Lu, Hong, and Terence D. Miethe. 2002. "Legal Representation and Criminal Processing in China." *British Journal of Criminology* 42, no. 2: 267–80.

Macauley, Melissa. 1998. *Social Power and Legal Culture: Litigation Masters in Late Imperial China*. Stanford: Stanford University Press.

Macbean, Nicola, and Elisa Nesossi. 2015. "Living up to Human Rights Responsibilities through Action: Lawyers and Law Firms in the Chinese Authoritarian Context." In *Human Rights Protection and Global Responsibilities*, eds. Kurt Mills and David Karp, pp. 180–200. Basingstoke, UK: Palgrave Macmillan.

MacCormack, Geoffrey. 1996. *The Spirit of Traditional Chinese Law*. Athens: University of Georgia Press.

MacCoun, Robert. 2005. "Voice, Control and Belonging: The Double-Edged Sword of Procedural Fairness." *Annual Review of Law and Social Science* 1: 171–201.

Mattis, Peter. 2012. "The Foundations of China's Future Stability." *Asia-Pacific Bulletin*, no. 149. http://www.eastwestcenter.org/sites/default/files/private/apb149_1.pdf.

McBarnett, Doreen. 1981. *Conviction: Law, the State and the Construction of the Police*. London: Macmillan.

McConville, Mike, Satnam Choongh, Pinky Choi Dick Wan, Eric Chui Wing Hong, Ian Dobinson, and Carol Jones. 2011. *Criminal Justice in China: An Empirical Inquiry*. Northampton, MA: Edward Elgar.

Meng Jinglin 门金玲. 2011. *Xingshi bianhu shiwu caocuo zhinan. Shangquan xing bian jiangyan yu fengxian tishi* 刑事辩护实务操作指南。尚权刑辩经验与风险提示 [*Guidance to Criminal Defence Mechanisms Operation. The Experience of the Shanquan Law Firm Criminal Defence and Risk Warnings*]. Beijing: Falü chubanshe.

Miao, Michelle. 2013. "Capital Punishment in China: A Populist Instrument of Social Governance." *Theoretical Criminology* 17, no. 2: 233–50.

Michelson, Ethan. 2003. "Unhooking from the State: Chinese Lawyers in Transition." PhD Dissertation, Department of Sociology, University of Chicago.

Michelson, Ethan. 2006. "The Practice of Law as an Obstacle to Justice: Chinese Lawyers at Work." *Law and Society Review* 40, no. 1: pp. 1–38.

Michelson, Ethan. 2007. "Lawyers, Political Embeddedness, and Institutional Continuity in China's Transition from Socialism." *American Journal of Sociology* 112, no. 2: pp. 352–414.

Michelson, Ethan, and Sida Liu. 2010. "What Do Chinese Lawyers Want? Political Values and Legal Practice." In *China's Emerging Middle Class: Beyond Economic Tranformation*, ed. Cheng Li, pp. 310–33. Washington: Brookings Institution Press.

Min Chunlei 闵春雷. 2002. "Lun xingxun bigong de chengxu ezhi 论刑讯逼供的程序遏制 [Discussion on the Procedures for Combating Extraction of Confession through Torture].” In *Kuxin ezhi lun* 酷刑遏制论 [*Discussion on Limiting Torture*], ed. Zhao Bingzhi 赵秉志, pp. 290–320. Beijing: Zhongguo renmin gong'an daxue chubanshe.

Minzner, Carl. 2013. “China at the Tipping Point? The Turn against Legal Reform.” *Journal of Democracy* 24, no. 1: 65–72.

Mou, Yu. 2017a. “The Constructed Truth: The Making of Police Dossiers in China.” *Social and Legal Studies* 26, no. 1: 69–88.

Mou, Yu. 2017b. “Overseeing Criminal Justice: The Supervisory Role of the Public Prosecution Service in China.” *Journal of Law and Society* 44, no. 4: 620–45.

MPS [Ministry of Public Security 公安部]. 2013. *Guanyu jin yibu jiaqiang xingshi zhifa ban'an gongzuo qieshi fangzhi fasheng yuanjia cuo'an de tongzhi* 关于进一步加强刑事执法办案工作切实防止发生冤假错案的通知 [*Notice on Further Strengthening and Improving the Work of Implementing the Law in Criminal Matters and Avoiding the Occurrence of Cases of Miscarriages of Justice*], June 5.

Nesossi, Elisa. 2012. *China's Pre-Trial Justice: Criminal Justice, Human Rights and Legal Reforms in Contemporary China*. London: Wildy, Simmonds and Hill.

Nesossi, Elisa. 2013. “Compromising for ‘Justice’? Criminal Proceedings and the Ethical Quandaries of Chinese Lawyers.” In *Criminal Justice in China. Comparative Perspectives*, eds. Mike McConville and Eva Pils, pp. 256–78. Cheltenham, UK: Edward Elgar Publishing.

Nesossi, Elisa. 2016. “The Politics of Torture and Miscarriages of Justice in Contemporary China.” *Journal of Comparative Law* 11, no. 2: 166–85.

Nesossi, Elisa. 2017. “Wrongful Convictions: The Useful Injustice?” In *Justice: The China Experience*, eds. Flora Sapio, Susan Trevaskes, Sarah Biddulph, and Elisa Nesossi, pp. 141–67. Cambridge: Cambridge University Press.

Nesossi, Elisa, and Ivan Franceschini. 2018. “Human Rights in the Age of Prosperity.” In *China Story Yearbook 2017: Prosperity*, eds. Jane Golley and Linda Jaivin, pp. 254–69. Canberra: ANU Press.

Nie Xiaosheng 聂晓生 and Jiang Jihai 江济海. 2002. “Guojian wo guo you xian chenmo quan zhidu de ji dian shexiang 构建我国有限沉默权制度的几点设想 [A Number of Assumptions on the Establishment of the Right to Silence System in China].” In Chenmo quan wenti yanjiu—Jianlun ruhe ezhi xingxun bigong 沉默权问题研究。兼论如何遏制刑讯逼供 [Research on the Issue of the Right to Silence—A Discussion on Ways to Limit Extraction of Confession through Torture], ed. Chen Guanzhong 陈光中, pp. 226–34. Beijing: Zhongguo renmin gong'an daxue chubanshe.

Ng, Kwai, and Xin He. 2016. “The Limits of Legal Commensuration: Blood Money and Negotiated Justice in China.” *American Journal of Sociology* 122, no. 4: 1104–43.

Ng, Kwai, and Xin He. 2017. *Embedded Court: Judicial Decision Making in China*. New York: Cambridge University Press.

Packer, Herbert. 1968. *Limits of the Criminal Sanctions*. Stanford: Stanford University Press.

Peerenboom, Randall. 1999. "Ruling the Country in Accordance with Law: Reflections on the Rule of Law in Contemporary China." *Cultural Dynamics* 11, no. 3: 315–51.

Peerenboom, Randall. 2015. "Fly High the Banner of Socialist Rule of Law with Chinese Characteristics! What Does the 4th Plenum Decision Mean for Legal Reforms in China?" *Hague Journal on the Rule of Law* 7, no. 1: 49–74.

Pei Cangling 裴苍龄. 1998. "Lun tuiding 论推定 [On Presumptions]." *Zhengfa luntan* 政法论坛 [*Tribune of Political Science and Law*], no. 4: 52–57.

Pei Zhiyong 裴智勇. 2003. "Zhili chaoqi jiya rengxu nuli 治理超期羁押仍须努力 [More Efforts Are Needed to Regulate Overdue Police Custody]." *Renmin ribao* 人民日报 [*People's Daily*], August 7: 10.

Pei Zhiyong 裴智勇. 2010. "Wanshan zhengju fazhi fangzhi yuanjia cuo'an 完善证据法治防止冤假错案 [Improving the Evidentiary System and Avoiding Miscarriages of Justice]." *Renmin ribao* 人民日报 [*People's Daily*]. June 2. http://news.163.com/10/0602/08/685MoIJJ000146BD.html.

People's Daily 人民日报. 2008. "Zhonggong zhongyang zhengzhiju zhaokai huiyi fenxi yanjiu 2008 nian jingji gongzuo he taolun shenhua sifa tizhi gaige gongzuo: Hu Jintao zhuchi 中共中央政治局召开会议分析研究 2008 年经济工作和讨论深化司法体制改革工作 胡锦涛主持 [The CCP Politburo Convened 2008 Conference on Economic Work and Discussed Optimizing Justice System Reform Work: Hu Jintao Chairs the Conference]." *Renmin ribao* 人民日报 [*People's Daily*]. November 29. http://cpc.people.com.cn/GB/64093/64094/8432810.html.

Pils, Eva. 2007. "Asking the Tiger for His Skin: Activism in China." *Fordham International Law Journal* 30: 1209–87.

Pils, Eva. 2014. *China's Human Rights Lawyers: Advocacy and Resistance*. Abington, UK: Routledge.

Pils, Eva. 2017. "A New Torture in China." *China Policy Institute: Analysis*, August 10. https://cpianalysis.org/2017/08/10/a-new-torture-in-china/.

Political Department of the Ministry of Public Security 公安部政治部. 1992. *Fandui xingxun bigong: anlie xuanbian* 反对刑讯逼供。案例选编 [*Combating the Extraction of Confession through Torture: A Collection of Cases*]. Beijing: Qunzhong chubanshe [For internal circulation].

Quirk, Hannah. 2010. *The Right of Silence. Principle, Pragmatism and Policy Making*. London: Routledge.

Rawls, John. 1971. *A Theory of Justice*. Cambridge, MA: Harvard University Press.

Rosenzweig, Joshua. 2011. "Lawyers Express Criticism of Criminal Procedure Law Revision Draft." CRJ Occasional Paper, August 31. http://www.siweiluozi.net/2011/08/lawyers-express-criticism-of-criminal.html.

Rosenzweig, Joshua. 2013. "Disappearing Justice: Public Opinion, Secret Arrest and Criminal Procedure Reform in China." *The China Journal* 70: 73–94.

Rosenzweig, Joshua. 2017. "State, Society, and the Justice Debate in Contemporary China." In *Justice: The China Experience*, eds. Flora Sapio, Susan Trevaskes, Elisa Nesossi, and Sarah Biddulph, pp. 26–66. Cambridge: Cambridge University Press.

Rosenzweig, Joshua, Flora Sapio, Jiang Jue, Teng Biao, and Eva Pils. 2013. "Comments on the 2012 Revision of the Chinese Criminal Procedure Law." In *Comparative Perspectives on Criminal Justice in China*, ed. Mike McConville and Eva Pils, pp. 455–503. Cheltenham, UK: Edward Elgar.

Safeguards Defenders. 2018. "Scripted and Staged: Behind the Scenes of China's Forced TV Confessions." APO, April 10. http://apo.org.au/node/141086/.

Sapio, Flora. 2008. "*Shuanggui* and Extralegal Detention in China." *China Information* 22, no. 1: 7–37.

Sapio, Flora. 2010. *Sovereign Power and the Law in China*. Leiden: Brill.

Sapio, Flora, Susan Trevaskes, Elisa Nesossi, and Sarah Biddulph. 2017. "The Expression of Justice in China." In *Justice: The China Experience*, ed. Flora Sapio, Susan Trevaskes, Elisa Nesossi, and Sarah Biddulph, pp. 3–26. Cambridge: Cambridge University Press.

Seppanen, Samuli. 2014. "Ideological Renewal and Nostalgia in China's Avant-Garde Scholarship." *Washington University Global Studies Law Review* 13, no. 1: 83–125.

Seppanen, Samuli. 2016. *Ideological Conflict and the Rule of Law in Contemporary China: Useful Paradoxes*. Cambridge: Cambridge University Press.

Seppanen, Samuli. 2017. "Rawls Rejected, Ignored and Radicalised." In *Justice: The China Experience*, eds. Flora Sapio, Susan Trevaskes, Elisa Nesossi, and Sarah Biddulph, pp. 26–66. Cambridge: Cambridge University Press.

Shan Yuxiao 单玉晓. 2016. "'Shenpan zhongxin' xingsu gaige luodi tixian fazhi jingshen qidai xihua luoshi 审判中心刑诉改革落地体现法治精神期待细化落实 ['Trial Centeredness' Criminal Procedure Embodies Spirit of Rule of Law and Should Receive Detailed Implementation]. *Caixin* 财新 [Caixin News], August 3.

She Meng 杜萌. 2007a. "2,829 ge jianchayuan shixing xunwen tongbu luyin luxiang 2829 个检察院实行讯问同步录音录像 [2,829 Procuratorates Have Implemented Audiovisual Recording during Interrogations]." *Fazhi ribao* 法制日报 [*Legal Daily*], November 14: 1.

She Meng 杜萌. 2007b. "Quancheng tongbu luyin luxiang: yiba fengli de shuangrenjian 全程同步录音录像: 一把锋利的双刃剑 [The Double-Edged Sword of Full Synchronization Audiovisual Recording]." *Fazhi ribao* 法制日报 [*Legal Daily*], November 21: 8.

Shen Deyong 沈德咏. 2015. "Lun yishenpan wei zhongxin de susong zhidu gaige 论以审判为中心的诉讼制度改革 [Placing the Trial at the Center of Procedural Law Reform]." *Zhongguo faxue* 中国法学 [*Chinese Jurisprudence*], no. 3: 5–6.

Sheng, Yi. 2003. "A Promise Unfulfilled: The Impact of China's 1996 Criminal Procedure Reform on China's Criminal Defence Lawyers' Role at the Pretrial Stage (Part 2)." *Perspectives* 4, no. 4: pp. 1–18.

Shi Mu 施木. 2001. "Wuzui tuiding: women zuo de yuanyuan bugou 无罪推定: 我们做得远不够 [Presumption of Innocence: What We Have Done Is Far from Enough]." *Renmin ribao* 人民日报 [*People's Daily*], October 10: 10.

Shi, Yanan. 2008. "On Restorative Justice Practiced in China: Status Quo, Challenge and the Future of Victim-Offender Reconciliation." *Frontiers of Law in China* 3, no. 2: 294–323.

Song Yinghui 宋英辉. 2007. *Xingshi susongfa* 刑事诉讼法 [*Criminal Procedure Law*]. Beijing: Qinghua daxue chubanshe.

Song Yinghui 宋英辉 and Wang Zhenhui 王贞会. 2010. "Woguo feifa zhengju paichu guize jiqi yunyong 我国非法证据排除规则及其适用 [Analysis on the Exclusionary Rules of Illegally Obtained Evidence and Its Application in China]." *Faxue zazhi* 法学杂志 [*Legal Science Magazine*], Issue 7: 15–18.

SPC [Supreme People's Court 最高人民法院]. 2013. "Zuigao renmin fayuan guanyu qieshi jianxing sifaweimin dali jiaqiang gongzheng sifa buduan tigao sifa gongxinli de ruogan yijian 最高人民法院关于切实践行司法为民，大力加强公正司法，不断提高司法公信力的若干意见 [Several Opinions on Actual Justice Practice for the People, Vigorously Strengthening a Fair Judiciary and Continuously Increasing Judicial Credibility]." September 6. http://legal.china.com.cn/2013-10/28/content_30426034.htm.

SPC [Supreme People's Court 最高人民法院]. 2017. "Zuigao renmin fayuan guanyu quanmian tuijin yishenpan weizhongxin de xingshi susong zhidu gaige de shishi yijian 最高人民法院关于全面推进以审判为中心的刑事诉讼制度改革的实施意见 [Implementation Opinions of the Supreme People's Court on Comprehensively Advancing a Trial-Centered Reform in the Criminal Procedure System]." February 2. http://www.court.gov.cn/zixun-xiangqing-36422.html.

SPC Monitor. 2016. "What China's Judicial Reform White Paper Says about Its Vision for Judiciary." *Supreme People's Court Monitor*, April 12. https://supremepeoplescourtmonitor.com/2016/04/12/what-chinas-judicial-reform-white-paper-says-about-its-vision-for-its-judiciary/.

SPC Monitor. 2017. "Supreme People's Court Ramps up its Judicial Responsibility System." *Supreme People's Court Monitor*, August 13. https://supremepeoplescourtmonitor.com/2017/08/13/supreme-peoples-court-ramps-up-its-judicial-responsibility-system/.

Sun Jibin 孙继斌. 2011. "Xingshi bianhu 'san nan' weihe bian 'shi nan' 刑事辩护三难为何变十难 [How Three Difficulties of Criminal Defense Became Ten Difficulties]." *Fazhi zhouwei* 法治周末 [*Legal Weekly*], January 20. http://www.legaldaily.com

.cn/zmbm/content/2011-01/20/content_2447577.htm?node=20350. [Translation in *Duihua Journal*, https://www.duihuahrjournal.org/2011/02/translation-how-three-difficulties-of.html.]

Tang Jinzong 唐锦宗. 2007. "Sifa gongzheng yu shehui wending wenti yanjiu 司法公正与社会稳定问题研究 [The Study of Judicial Justice and Social Stability]." *Xueshu tansuo* 学术探索 [*Scholarly Exploration*], no. 6: 75–80.

Tanner, Harold M. 1999. *Strike Hard! Anti-Crime Campaigns and Chinese Criminal Justice 1979–1989*. Ithaca: East Asian Program, Cornell University.

Tanner, Murray S. 2000. "State Coercion and the Balance of Awe: The 1983–1986 'Stern Blows' Anti-Crime Campaign." *The China Journal* 44: 93–125.

Tanner, Murray S. 2005. "Campaign-Style Policing in China and Its Critics." In *Crime, Punishment, and Policing in China*, ed. Borge Bakken, pp. 171–88. Lanham, MD: Rowman and Littlefield.

Tanner, Murray S. 2013. "Internal Security." In *Handbook of China's Governance and Domestic Politics*, ed. Chris Ogden, pp. 88–96. Florence, KY: Routledge.

Tian Wenchang 田文昌. 1999. "Lifa jiazhi quxiang fasheng bianhua 立法价值取向发生变化 [The Orientation for Legislative Value Is Changing]." *Renmin ribao* 人民日报 [*People's Daily*], August 18: 9.

Tian Wenchang 田文昌. 2007. "Xingshi susong zhong lüshi mianlin de kunhuo 刑事诉讼中律师面临的困惑 [The Difficulties Encountered by Lawyers during Criminal Proceedings]. In *Lüshi yu fazhi* 律师与法制 [*Lawyers and the Rule of Law*], pp. 201–09. Beijing: Zhongguo zhengfa daxue chubanshe.

Trevaskes, Susan. 2007. *Courts and Criminal Justice in Contemporary China*. Lanham, MD: Lexington Press.

Trevaskes, Susan. 2009. "Restorative Justice or McJustice with Chinese Characteristics?" In *Twenty-First Century China: Views from Australia*, ed. Mary Farquhar, pp. 77–96. Cambridge: Cambridge Scholars.

Trevaskes, Susan. 2010. *Policing Serious Crime in China: From "Strike Hard" to "Kill Fewer."* London: Routledge.

Trevaskes, Susan. 2011. "Political Ideology, the Party, and Politicking: Justice Reform in China." *Modern China* 37, no. 3: 315–44.

Trevaskes, Susan. 2012. *The Death Penalty in Contemporary China*. New York: Palgrave Macmillan.

Trevaskes, Susan. 2012. "The Ideology of Law and Order." In *Red Rising Red Eclipse: China Story Yearbook 2012*, ed. Geremie R. Barmé, pp. 60–83. Canberra: Australian Centre on China in the World, Australian National University.

Trevaskes, Susan. 2018. "The Death Penalty and Human Rights." *Handbook of Human Rights in China*, eds. Sarah Biddulph and Joshua Rosenzweig. Cheltenham, UK: Edward Elgar (forthcoming).

Trevaskes, Susan, and Elisa Nesossi. 2014. "Under Rule of Law." In *Civilising China: China Story Yearbook 2013*, ed. Geremie R. Barmé and Jeremy Goldkorn, pp. 202–29. Canberra: Australian Centre on China in the World, Australian National University.

Trevaskes, Susan, Elisa Nesossi, Sarah Biddulph and Flora Sapio. 2014. "Framing the Stability Imperative." In *The Politics of Law and Stability in China*, ed. Susan Trevaskes, Elisa Nesossi, Sarah Biddulph, and Flora Sapio, pp. 269–83. Cheltenham, UK: Edward Elgar.

Tyler, Tom R. 1990. *Why People Obey the Law: Procedural Justice, Legitimacy, and Compliance*. New Haven: Yale University Press.

Tyler, Tom R., and E. Allan Lind. 2001. "Procedural Justice." In *Handbook of Justice Research in Law*, eds. Joseph Sanders and V. Lee Hamilton, pp. 65–92. New York: Kluwer.

United Nations, Commission on Human Rights, Civil and Political Rights, Including the Question of Torture and Detention. 2006. *Report of the Special Rapporteur on Torture and Other Cruel, Inhuman or Degrading Treatment or Punishment, Manfred Nowak. Mission to China*, E/CN4/2006/6/Add6.

Van Rooij, Benjamin. 2014. "Regulation by Escalation: Unrest, Lawmaking, and Law Enforcement in China." In *The Politics of Law and Stability in China*, ed. Susan Trevaskes, Elisa Nesossi, Flora Sapio, and Sarah Biddulph, pp. 83–107. Cheltenham, UK: Edward Elgar.

Walker, Laurens, E., Allan Lind, and John Thibaut. 1979. "The Relation between Procedural and Distributive Justice." *Virginia Law Review* 65, no. 8: 1401–20.

Wang, Chenguang. 2010. "From the Rule of Man to the Rule of Law." In *China's Journey Toward the Rule of Law: Legal Reform, 1978–2008*, eds. Cai Dingjian and Wang Chenguang, pp. 1–50. Leiden: Brill.

Wang Gangping 王钢平, ed. 1997. *Xingxun bigong zui* 刑讯逼供罪 [*The Crime of Extracting Confession through Torture*]. Beijing: Zhongguo jiancha chubanshe.

Wang Guanxian 王光贤. 2007. *Jinzhi kuxing de lilun yu shixian: guoji he guonei jiandu jizhi xiang jiehe de shijiao* 禁止酷刑的理论与实现: 国际和国内监督机制相结合的视角 [*Theory and Practice on the Prohibition of Torture: Perspectives on the Combination of the International and Domestic Supervisory Mechanisms*]. Shanghai: Shanghai shiji chuban jituan.

Wang Jian 王戬. 2015. "Lun 'paichu heli huiyi' zhengming biaozhun de Zhongguo yiyi 论'排除合理怀疑证明标准的中国意义 [On the Significance of the 'Beyond Reasonable Doubt' Standard of Proof in China]." *Huadong zhengfa daxue xuebao* 华东政法大学学报 [*Journal of Huadong University of Politics and Law*], no. 6: 103–14.

Wang Lili 王丽丽. 2008. "Xingsu fa bu gai lüshi fa nan shixing 刑诉法不改律师法难实行 [If the Criminal Procedure Law Will Not Be Revised, Would It Be Difficult to Put in Practice the Lawyers Law?]." *Jiancha ribao* 检察日报 [*Procuratorial Daily*], March 12: 5–6.

Wang Lili 王丽丽 and Meng Chufei 孟澍菲. 2008. "Xin lüshi fa: jiao hao zhi hou hai you yinyou 新律师法叫好之后还有隐忧 [Lawyers Law: After Having Been Applauded There Remain Hidden Concerns]." *Jiancha ribao* 检察日报 [*Procuratorial Daily*], January 21: 6.

Wang Limin 王立民. 2007. "'Sifa hexie' yu 'sifa gongzheng' bianxi 司法和谐与司法公正辨析 [Distinguishing between Judicial Harmony and Judicial Justice]." *Sohu News*, January 25. http://star.news.sohu.com/20070125/n247832524.shtml.

Wang Limin 王立民. 2006. "The Achievements and Prospects for Court Reform in China." *Frontiers of Law in China* 1, no. 1: 1–13.

Wang Minyuan 王敏远. 2011. "Lun weichengnianren xingshi susong chengxu 论未成年人刑事诉讼程序 [Juvenile Criminal Procedure]." *Zhongguo faxue* 中国法学 [*Chinese Legal Science*], no. 6: 61–68.

Wang Shumao 王树茂. 2015. "Feifa zhengju paichu guize de sifa shiyong bianxi 非法证据排除规则的司法实用辨析 [Differentiate and Analyze the Judicial Use of the Rules on the Exclusion of Illegal Evidence]." *Zhengzhi yu falü* 政治与法律 [*Politics and Law*], no. 7: 151–61.

Wang Xinyou 王新友. 2007a. "Fanshi xunwen quancheng luxiang. Jun wei faxian weifa ban'an 凡是讯问全程录像。均未发现违法办案 [The Overall Application of Visual Recording. Almost No Illegalities in Handling Cases]." *Jiancha ribao* 检察日报 [*Procuratorial Daily*], November 14: 1.

Wang Xinyou 王新友. 2007b. "Quancheng luxiang tuxian si da gongxiao 全程录像凸显四大贡献 [Overall Visual Recording Displays Four Main Benefits]." *Jiancha ribao* 检察日报 [*Procuratorial Daily*], November 15: 1.

Wang Yongkuan 王永宽. 1991. *Zhongguo gudai kuxing: Zhongguo chuantong wenhua toushi* 中国古代酷刑: 中国传统文化透视 [*Torture in Ancient China: A Perspective on Chinese Traditional Culture*]. Zhengzhou: Zhengzhou guji chubanshe.

Wen Zhengbang 文正邦 and Sun Hongkun 孙洪坤. 2000. "Wuzui tuiding de fazhexue sikao 无罪推定的法哲学思考 [Think of Presumption of Innocence in Philosophy of Law]." *Fa shang yanjiu* 法商研究 [*Studies in Law and Business*], no. 2: 53–58.

Wang, Zhuhao, and David Caruso. 2017. "Is an Oral-Evidence-Based Criminal Trial Possible in China?" *International Journal of Evidence and Proof* 21, nos. 1–2: 52–68.

Wang, Zhuhao, and Li Jia. 2014. "Interactions between National Judicial Practice and Supernational Legal Values: Reflections on China's Evidence Legislation Development." *China Legal Science* 2, no. 6: 118–41.

Woo, Margaret and Mary Gallager, eds. 2011. *Chinese Justice: Civil Dispute Resolution in Contemporary China*. New York NY: Cambridge University Press.

Wu Xiaofeng 武小凤 and Liu Jinlin 刘金林. 2007. "San xiang zhidu ke yufang xingxun bigong 三项制度可预防刑讯逼供 [Three Measures That Can Prevent the Extraction of Confessions through Torture]." *Jiancha ribao* 检查日报 [*Procuratorial Daily*] December 18: 3.

Wu Danhong 吴丹红. 2004. “Juese, qingjing, yu shehui rongren: fashehuixue shiye zhong de xingxun bigong 角色、情境与社会容忍: 法社会学视野中的刑讯逼供 [Roles, Context and Social Tolerance: The Extraction of Confession from Torture from a Social-Legal Perspective].” *Zhongwai faxue* 中外法学 [*Peking University Law Journal*] 18, no. 2: 147–69.

Wu Hongyao 吴宏耀. 2014. “Feifa zhengju paichu de guize yu shixiao: jianlun woguo feifa zhengju paichu guize de wanshan jinlu 非法证据排除的规则与实效: 兼论我国非法证据排除规则的完善进路 [The Suppression of Illegally Obtained Evidence: Rule and Effectiveness].” *Xiandai faxue* 现代法学 [*Modern Legal Science*] 36, no. 4: 121–30.

Xi, Jinping. 2015. “Accelerating the Establishment of Socialist Rule of Law in China.” *Qiushi Journal* (*English Edition*) 7, no. 1 (March 16).

Xiao Peiquan 肖沛权. 2015. “Paichu heli huaiyi jiqi Zhongguo shiyong 排除合理怀疑及其中国适用 [Beyond Reasonable Doubt and Its Application in China].” *Zhengfa luntan* 政法论坛 [*Tribune of Political Science and Law*] 33, no. 6: 51–64.

Xinhua. 2017a. “China Focus: China Scores New Achievements in Judicial Protection of Human Rights.” *Xinhua*, July 15. http://news.xinhuanet.com/english/2017-07/15/c_136446475.htm.

Xinhua. 2017b. “China's Comprehensive Moves in Advancing Rule of Law.” *Xinhua*. August 11.

Xiong Qiuhong 熊秋红. 1997. “Lun xinshi bianhu zhidu zhi lilun jichu (shang) 论刑事辩护制度之理论基础 (上) [On Theoretical Bases of the Criminal Defense System (Part I)].” *Zhengfa luntan* 政法论坛 [*Tribune of Political Science and Law*], Issue 1: 41–48, 58.

Xu Jingcun 徐静村. 2003. *Ershiyi shiji Zhongguo xingshi chengxu gaige yanjiu: ‘Zhonghua renmin gongheguo xingshi susongfa’ di'er xiuzhengan* (*Xuezhe jianyigao*) 《21世纪中国刑事程序改革研究: <中华人民共和国刑事诉讼法>第二修正案(学者建议稿)》 [*Research on 21st Century China's Criminal Procedure Reform: Second Amendment to the Criminal Procedure Law of the People's Republic of China* (*Proposal by Scholars*)]. Beijing: Falü chubanshe.

Xu Jun 徐隽. 2013. “Sifa tizhi gaige zhongdian tupo 司法体制改革重点突破 [Critical Breakthroughs in Judicial System Reform].” *Renmin ribao* 人民日报 [*People's Daily*], December 25: 18.

Xu Xin 徐昕. 2010. “Panting Li Zhuang an er shen 旁听李庄案二审 [Observing the Second Trial of the Li Zhuang Case].” Law blog. http://justice.fyfz.cn/art/579232.htm.

Yang, Kai. 2016. “The Construction of Preventive Mechanism for Wrongful Convictions from the Perspective of Trial-Centered Doctrine.” *China Legal Science* 4, no. 3: 5–28.

Yang Weixing 杨卫星. 2008. “Ruhe chuli xin lüshi fa yu xingsu fa de chongtu 如何处理新律师法与刑诉法的冲突 [How to Solve the Contradictions between the New

Lawyers Law and the Criminal Procedure Law].” *Renmin fayuan bao* 人民法院报 [*Journal of the People's Court*], April 18: 5.

Yang, Yuguan, and Chen Zinan. 2015. “On the Question of Exclusionary Rule in China.” *China Legal Science* 3: 3–23.

Ye Qing 叶青 and Gu Yuejin 顾跃进. 2005. *Zhongguo lüshi zhidu yanjiu* 中国律师制度研究 [Study of the Lawyers' System in China]. Shanghai: Shanghai shehui kexue chubanshe.

Yi, Yanyou. 2012. “State Ideology Transition and Procedure Model Reformation: China's Criminal Procedure Law and Its Revisions.” *Tsinghua China Law Review* 4: 155–222.

Yin Jianfeng 阴剑锋. 2011. “Lun falü xiaoguo yu shehui xiaoguo de tongyi: yi guanche kuanyan xiangji xingshi zhengce wei zhongxing 论法律效果与社会效果的统一：以贯彻宽严相济刑事政策为中心 [On the Unification of Legal Effect and Social Effect: From the Perspective of the Implementation of the Criminal Policy of Combining Leniency and Harshness].” *Henan shehui kexue* 河南社会科学 [*Henan Social Science*] 19, no. 2: 87–90.

Yu, Ping. 2002. “Glittery Promise vs Dismal Reality: The Role of Criminal Lawyer in the People's Republic of China After the 1996 Revision of the Criminal Procedure Law.” *Vanderbilt Journal of Transnational Law* 35, no. 3: 827–65.

Yu, Xingzhong. 1989. “Legal Pragmatism in the People's Republic of China.” *Journal of Chinese Law* 3, no. 1: 29–51.

Zhang Zipei 张子培. 1983. “Ping ‘wuzui tuiding’ 评 无罪推定 [Review on ‘Presumption of Innocence].” *Zhongguo zhengfa daxue xuebao* 中国政法大学学报 [*Journal of the Chinese University of Politics and Law*], no. 4: 19–22.

Zhang, Baosheng. n.d. “Reflecting on Development of Evidence Law in China.” Working paper. https://www.bu.edu/ilj/files/2015/03/Baosheng-Zhang-Reflecting-on-Development-of-Evidence-Law-in-China.pdf.

Zhang, Baosheng and Fei Zheng. 2014. “Reforming the Criminal Evidence System in China.” *Asian Journal of Criminology* 9, no. 2: 103–24.

Zhang, Baosheng, and Jia Cao. 2017. “The Mirror of Evidence and the Plausibility of Judicial Proof.” *International Journal of Evidence and Proof* 21, nos. 1–2: 119–32.

Zhang, Qianfan. 2016. “Judicial Reform in China.” In *China's Socialist Rule of Law Reforms under Xi Jinping*, eds. John Garrick and Yan Chang Benne, pp. 17–29. London: Routledge.

Zhao Bingzhi 赵秉志. 2003. *Kuxing ezhi lun* 酷刑遏制论 [*Discussion on Limiting Torture*]. Beijing: Zhongguo renmin gong'an daxue chubanshe.

Zhao, Bingzhi, and Zhijun Chen. 2013. “The Fate of the Theory of Social Harm in contemporary China.” In *Renmin Chinese Law Review: Selected Papers of the Jurist*, Vol. 1, ed. Jichun Shi, pp. 133–58. Cheltenham, UK: Edward Elgar.

Zhao, Yanrong. 2017. “The Courts' Active Role in the Striving for Judicial Independence in China.” *Frontiers of Law in China* 12, no. 2: 278–309.

Zhongguo Ribao 中国日报. 2017. “Zuigaofa Shen Deyong: Rang redian anjian chengwei quanmin gongxiang de fazhi gongkaike 最高法沈德咏: 让热点案件成为全民共享的法治公开课 Shen Deyong from the SPC: Let Highlighted Cases Become Open Lectures of Rule of Law for the General Public].” *Zhongguo ribao* 中国日报 [*China Daily*], April 5. http://www.court.gov.cn/zixun-xiangqing-39292.html.

Zhou, Bin 周斌. 2016. “Faxue zhuanjia jiedu tuijin yishenpan wei zhongxin de xingshi susong zhidu gaige yijian 法学专家解读推进以审判为中心的刑事诉讼制度改革意见 [Legal Experts Explained the Opinion on Advancing a Trial-Centered Reform in the Criminal Procedure System].” *Fazhi ribao* 法制日报 [*Legal Daily*], October 10. http://www.legaldaily.com.cn/index_article/content/2016-10/10/content_6831148.htm.

Zhou Guojun 周国均. 1999. “Yanjin xingxun bigong ruogan wenti tantao 严禁刑讯逼供若干问题探讨 [Discussion of Several Issues Concerning the Prohibition of the Extraction of Confession through Torture].” *Zhengfa luntan* 政法论坛 [*Tribune of Political Science and Law*], no. 1: 82–95.

Zhu, Sanzhu. 2004. “Reforming State Institutions: Privatizing the Lawyers’ System.” In *Governance in China*, ed. Howell Jude, pp. 58–76. Oxford: Rowman and Littlefield.

Zhu, Weijiu. 2010. “Towards Governance by Rule of Law.” In *China’s Journey toward the Rule of Law: Legal Reform 1978–2008*, eds. Dingjian Cai and Chenguang Wang, pp. 101–54. Leiden: Brill.

Zuo Weimin 左为民. 2016. “Jianquan fengong zeren, huxiang peihe, huxiang zhiyue yuanze de sikao 健全分工责任, 互相配合, 互相制约原则的思考 [Reflections on the Principle of Dividing Labor and Responsibilities, Mutually Coordinate, and Mutually Restrain]. *Fazhi yu shehui fazhan* 法制与社会发展 [*The Legal System and Social Development*] 2: 25–30.

Zuo, Weimin 左为民. 2017. “An Empirical Study of the Chinese Criminal File System: Focusing on the File of Evidence.” Available at https://papers.ssrn.com/sol3/papers.cfm?abstract_id=2869635.

Zuo Weimin 左卫民 and Zhou Hongbo 周洪波. 2002. “Cong hefa dao feifa: xingxun bigong deyujing fenxi 从合法到非法-刑讯逼供的语境分析 [From Legal to Illegal: The Contextual Analysis of the Extraction of Confession through Torture].” *Faxue* 法学 [*Legal Science*], no. 10: 31–40.

www.ingramcontent.com/pod-product-compliance
Lightning Source LLC
Chambersburg PA
CBHW031330230926
51848CB00001B/168
9789004386372